# CATHY LECHNER

# Couldn't We Just Kill 'em and Tell God They Died?

## Overcoming Difficult Relationships With Your Family and Friends

CREATION
HOUSE
Orlando, FL

Creation House
Strang Communications Company
600 Rinehart Road
Lake Mary, FL 32746
Phone: 407-333-3132
Fax: 407-333-7100
Web site: http://www.creationhouse.com

Unless otherwise noted, all Scripture quotations are from
the King James Version of the Bible.

Scripture quotations marked AMP are from the Amplified Bible.
Old Testament copyright © 1965, 1987 by the Zondervan Corporation.
The Amplified New Testament copyright © 1954, 1958, 1987 by the
Lockman Foundation. Used by permission.

Scripture quotations marked MSG are from The Message. Copyright © 1993,
1994, 1995, 1996. Used by permission of NavPress Publishing Group.

Scripture quotations marked NAS are from the New American Standard Bible.
Copyright © 1960, 1962, 1963, 1968, 1971, 1972, 1973, 1975, 1977 by the
Lockman Foundation. Used by permission.

Scripture quotations marked NIV are from the Holy Bible,
New International Version. Copyright © 1973, 1978, 1984, International Bible
Society. Used by permission.

Scripture quotations marked RSV are from the Revised Standard Version of the
Bible. Copyright © 1946, 1952, 1971 by the Division of Christian Education of
the National Council of the Churches of Christ in the USA. Used by permission.

Scripture quotations marked TLB are from The Living Bible.
Copyright © 1971. Used by permission of Tyndale House Publishers Inc.,
Wheaton, IL 60189. All rights reserved.

This book is lovingly dedicated to two people who have managed to maintain a relationship with me for forty-one years — my parents — Rose and Clive Rothert.

You gave, stretched yourself, sacrificed and often went an extra mile to raise three children, pastor the church and each work two jobs — all at the same time. You poured out your lives and yet, after forty-eight years, your love for the Lord and each other is still growing — amazing!

# Acknowledgements

Writing a book is really hard work. It takes enormous discipline and a lot of time to bring it all together in a way that makes sense. In the natural, I possess few of these qualities. That is all the more reason I needed to thank these awesome people who have worked so very hard to make this book a reality.

Randi, my beloved husband, you inspire me, teach me, help me and even provoke me. Only in eternity will others realize your value and anointing. We will be partners forever.

My wonderful children, this is the legacy that mommy will leave to you: that you must serve your God with gladness and joy.

Jerusha Rose, you are every mother's dream of what a daughter can be. You are my friend and my encourager.

Hannah Ruth, my beautiful princess and bath time buddy. How you can make me laugh, and not many people can do that.

Gabriel Levi, my caretaker, always giving and never taking. We can already see the Father's heart in you.

Samuel Josiah, nobody understands you but us. You always remind me why I hate to leave home.

Abagael Elisha, our surprise and our joy. You were aptly named. Your sweetness and love for your brothers and sisters are innocent. Let no one take that from you.

Lydia Danielle, it is a little too early to say what strong characteristics will propel you through life, but I think you may be a prophetic psalmist. Your nightly songs lift me from my slumber! I thank God every day for allowing me to be your mother.

Stephen and Joy Strang, I have been privileged to call you my friends. Thank you for challenging, sharpening and encouraging me to exceed my own expectations.

Tom Freiling, my publisher, the grace and faith of God that is in your life brought life to these books. And you are also a really nice guy. Rob, not only did you do a great job in marketing, but you are a wonderful tour guide, and you make me laugh. My sincere thanks to all the staff at Creation House who make me look good.

My pastors Wiley and Jeana Tomlinson and Bob and Mary Louise Bailey. I acknowledge God's wisdom and favor for establishing us at New Covenant Ministries.

Erin, my faithful secretary and best friend. You are the most godly example I know of the principles in this book. The next one's for you.

Not many people have paid the price that Lynn and Eric Jones have been willing to pay. Twice you left it all to follow the Lord's vision that He placed first in our hearts and then in yours.

My sweet Laura Lee O'Toole, God dropped you from heaven for such a time as this. Thank you for loving my children.

I am also grateful to Trudy Cooper and all those who serve the Lord and me so faithfully — especially our Covenant partners that so generously and sacrificially invest in this ministry.

Over the years God has given me favor in the eyes of many pastors that have stood with me and loved me — the good, the bad and the ugly. I would like to give a much overdue thank you to them. Pastors George and Elaine Cunard, Pastors Paul and Sharon Zink, Pastors Benny and Suzanne Hinn, Pastors Ron and Lynn Durham, Pastors Jesse and Lydell James, Pastors Mark and Stephanie Moder, Pastors Ferrell and Lynne Lister, Pastors Houston and Evelyn Miles, and my dear friend Freeda Bowers.

I would be remiss if I did not also thank those difficult people who thought they were my enemies. Thank you! The Lord used you to teach me the truths and principles found in this book.

To You, My Lord Jesus, be all the glory and all the honor and all the praise for desiring to have a relationship with me. Amazing!

# Contents

# 1

# Couldn't We Just Kill 'em and Tell God They Died?

I never seem to say the right thing. Actually I believe I do, but others take my words the wrong way or twist them to mean something entirely different. Some people can be so immature. I find myself asking the question, "Couldn't we just kill 'em and tell God they died?"

One particular Sunday evening, I was well into my usual routine — rinsing each dish and practically throwing it into the dishwasher. I got the rinsing part from my mother, though I never could understand why I had to wash the dishes twice. Wasn't that the dishwasher's job? When I asked her why, I got a really intelligent answer. "There's no invisible hand in there that rubs the crud off the dishes and gets them clean," she said. Sad thing is, I find myself saying the same words to *my* daughter.

Anyway, while I was doing my thing with the dishes, I suddenly began to cry.

It had started out being a great Sunday. The service was anointed, and the message Randi gave was particularly encouraging. We were even out of church by 2:00 P.M.

We had dinner guests that afternoon, and after I served them iced tea and made them feel at home, I excused myself so I could change into more comfortable clothing.

Randi was already in our bedroom changing his clothes. Our conversation was sweet as we talked about the wonderful service we had that morning. We were looking forward to a wonderful time of fellowship with our guests. That's when disaster struck, in the form of my poodle.

Somehow our Bo (short for Beauregard) managed to push open the bedroom door, which was in sight of the living room. We looked up to see our astonished guests staring with raised eyebrows at my husband, clad only in his undershorts, socks and shoes. Mercifully I was still fully dressed, or those poor folks would have needed inner healing.

My normally sweet, kind husband lunged for the door, slammed it shut and then proceeded to yell at me in a decibel just below the sonic boom.

I was mortified. "You always leave the door open! You never shut the door!" he said.

I really hate those words: you always and you never. Mortified turned into really, really mad.

"How could you yell at me like that? It's just a little mistake," I yelled back.

"It wasn't you standing there in your green underwear and boots in plain view of church people!" he bellowed.

Things went from bad to worse — because I started to laugh. (It really was a funny sight.) Wrong move. I wondered what our visitors were thinking. Maybe, just maybe, they were embarrassed enough to leave. I peeked out the door. No, they were still there.

Being a very professional ministry couple, we put on a happy face and walked out of the bedroom, hand in hand, to host the potential church members. I wondered, *How could things go from heaven on earth in the morning service to not-so-heavenly in the space of half an hour?* I believe the answer is that we are human, and we all really need help!

That's why I chose to write this book on relationships. I don't have all the answers, but I do want to help you to love impossible people. Some friends we choose ourselves; however, other relationships are almost forced on us. I would like to share some relational principles with you — such as how to make an enemy your friend.

## The Way of Love

> If I speak with human eloquence and angelic ecstasy but don't love, I'm nothing but the creaking of a rusty gate. If I speak God's Word with power, revealing all His mysteries and making everything plain as day, and if I have faith that says to a mountain, "Jump" and it jumps, but I don't love, I'm nothing. If I give everything I own to the poor and even go to the stake to be burned as a martyr, but I don't love, I've gotten nowhere. So, no matter what I say, what I believe, and what I do, I'm bankrupt without love (1 Cor. 13:1-3, MSG).

A woman once told me, "My husband always brings me candy or flowers, but they don't mean much because he doesn't back it up with acts of love."

My first inclination was to ask her what kind of candy he brings her. My second was to smack her and say, *Do you know how many women wish their husbands would bring them candy or flowers?* But then I heard what she was really saying. Her husband was giving her what he thought would

10

make her happy, not what she really needed.

On our honeymoon, my groom and I stayed in a cabin in the hills of North Carolina. Gorgeous mountains surrounded us, and all you could hear were the sounds of chirping birds and the gurgling of a nearby stream. There was no one around for miles. I absolutely hated it. My idea of camping is staying at a Marriott, where the only sounds are the clanking of the room service dishes and the maid bringing in fresh towels.

One night Randi prepared dinner for me. It was a chicken that he had personally roasted in the fireplace, along with rice and broccoli. Parts of the chicken looked as though they had fallen into the fire, while other parts had light pink juices running out of them.

He was so happy with his gift to me. We hadn't been married long enough for him to realize that my all-time most hated dinner in the whole world was blackened, raw chicken, rice and broccoli. He just wanted to bless me, even though I didn't consider the meal a blessing. We learned a valuable lesson that night almost twenty-one years ago that has stuck with us: It is not a blessing if it is not what pleases you.

Many times we believe that if something pleases us, then it will surely please another. That is exactly how some people serve God. They give Him what they think He wants, instead of reading the Word and discovering what He really wants.

> A new commandment I give unto you, That ye love one another; as I have loved you, that ye also love one another (John 13:34).

God tells us how to love, because He realizes that we will love according to what seems right to the natural man and not to the spiritual man. In the movie *Love Story*, Ali MacGraw told Ryan O'Neal, "Love means never having to say you're sorry." When I heard that I started to cry in the dark movie theater. I was sixteen years old. My boyfriend at the time took my hand and, turning my face to his, said, "Yes, baby, that's true. Let's never forget that." Then we both cried as the theme music played on.

Many years later I can truthfully tell you that not only is that a stupid saying, but it's also a big fat lie. After twenty years of marriage, six children, three pastorates, two books, hundreds of conferences and four poodles, I can assure you that love is *continually* having to say you're sorry!

> Love never gives up.
> Loves cares more for others than for self.
> Love doesn't want what it doesn't have.
> Love doesn't strut,
> Doesn't have a swelled head,
> Doesn't force itself on others,
> Isn't always "me first,"
> Doesn't fly off the handle,
> Doesn't keep score of the sins of others,
> Doesn't revel when others grovel,
> Takes pleasure in the flowering of truth,
> Puts up with anything,
> Trusts God always,
> Always looks for the best,
> Never looks back,
> But keeps going to the end (1 Cor. 13:4-10, MSG).

Acts of love don't cost money, but they do require time, change and often sacrifice. We have seen supernatural attacks leveled against families in this generation — especially families who have little time and great resistance to change and sacrifice.

We need to "fight the good fight of faith" and tear down strongholds in our lives that would try to destroy our families, marriages, church, work and relationships. Every situation that might bring God's glory on the earth Satan will ultimately attack. What is his sole purpose? It's to divide us from one another, divorce us from our spouses and separate us from our church and pastors.

What are some practical principles that we can apply to our relationships in order to bring change and healing?

## Everyone Loves a Gift

Everyone loves a beautifully wrapped present. Have you ever been guilty of tearing the beautiful paper from a gift and reading the big letters on the box that revealed exactly what you have always wanted — only to open it and find out that even though the box came from Cashmere Sweaters, Inc., inside were Tupperware bowls?

Most people can see the disappointment on your face, even though you say "Thank you" after you have torn off the elaborate wrapping.

We must give one another lasting gifts, and they may cost us our lives.

> This is how much God loved the world: He gave
> His Son, his one and only Son (John 3:16, MSG).

## *A Gift of Changing My Behavior*

My husband is an open and talkative man. He wants to tackle disagreements and problems head on. It may take three hours to explore each detail and projected probable outcome. His motto: Let's talk it out, determine the mind of God and resolve each issue.

I, on the other hand, clam up. "Nothing is wrong" is often my reply. This is usually said through tight, tense lips, in response to something I don't agree with.

We have never allowed our children to scream, "I hate you!" or some other ugly exclamation and then run to their

13

room, slam the door, throw themselves on the bed and continue screaming. Instead we encourage them to talk to us and get understanding, even if it ultimately results in discipline. I don't want to pass on to my children the clam-up behavior. I'm sure their spouses will be grateful.

It has taken years of prayer and effort, but I am determined to give our marriage the gift of opening up when my husband asks. My honest and kind response is what Randi appreciates most and makes him feel valued.

What change would make your spouse, child or friend feel valued? If you are inclined to nag, why don't you give them all a present — no reminders for a whole week? This will require much prayer, because after only one day you might think you are going to explode.

Our willingness to change is one of the greatest gifts we can give to a friend (or an enemy).

## A Gift of Companionship

In impending divorces, often the husband complains that his wife never does anything with him that he enjoys.

A pastor's wife was having severe marital problems. I had known this couple several years and had observed their ministry and their personal relationship. As she poured out her heart to me, she insisted that divorce was their only option.

I am not a psychologist, a professional counselor or even a *Brady Bunch* wife and mother. I reminded her of this fact. But I told her what I had observed as an outsider. I told her that she was no fun. All she talked about was demons and church problems. She made serving the Lord sound like a burden instead of a blessing. She had become so spiritual, she never laughed anymore.

The Word says, "Go, eat of the fat, drink of the sweet, and send portions to him who has nothing prepared...for the joy of the Lord is your strength" (Neh. 8:10, NAS).

"Eat the fat" has got to mean cake. Drink the sweet

sounds like a Coke to me. God is telling us that we need to have a party now and then. Nehemiah had been in a building program for a long time. Talk about being stressed out! God knew that he and the Israelites needed a break from the labor and the battle.

My friend argued that someone needed to be responsible and concerned and do warfare and so on. I reminded her that she had fretted, fasted, prayed, nagged and analyzed the problem nearly to death. Her husband had not changed, but she had — and not for the better. I said, "God can either fix the situation, or He can't. God knows your heart. Now it's time to relax, love your husband and, though you may feel that celebrating and laughing are inappropriate behaviors relative to the severity of your problems, you need to engage in them to exercise your faith."

She promised she would try. God honored her faltering steps of faith. It works, my friend. That was twelve years ago, and her marriage is strong.

Author Willard F. Harley, Jr., who wrote *His Needs, Her Needs,* stated: "It's imperative that marriage partners experience their most enjoyable recreational moments with each other."

May I suggest that you invite your mate out for coffee? Ask him to list the top ten things that add to his enjoyment. This will require a sacrifice of your time and interests, especially if five of his favorite pastimes include the TV, the recliner, the newspaper, a cold drink and a good burp!

Singles, stop playing the same recording of loneliness. Don't wait for someone to reach out to you. Make an effort to be a blessing to others. If you are bored beyond measure, you can come to my house. We have plenty of diapers to change.

## Take the Initiative

For a long time I griped because I was the one who had to pay the bills. I was sick and tired of being the one who had to see how much we owed, balance the checkbook and figure out how we could buy six pairs of shoes with what was left. I fussed until one day I faced the facts that I was better at doing this than my husband was and that I needed to do it without complaining. I am Randi's help-mate. One of the highest compliments a husband can pay his wife is to trust her with the checkbook.

## What About Sex?

This portion is for married people only. Be sexually aggressive some of the time. Your mate longs to believe that he is wonderful enough for you to yearn for his sexual companionship.

It means everything to a man if he has a home where he knows he is of inestimable value. Your husband can stand much more of the rough and tumble of a cutthroat world if you have convinced him that his home is an emotional center where he is vitally important.

## A Special Thoughtfulness

It had been a rough night. My plane was two and a half hours late arriving from Charlotte, and I had a cold. Two of the babies had been up most of the night. My husband had an early morning meeting, so I got up and served him breakfast.

"Why are you being so nice to me?" he questioned. My reply was, "Because I want you to stay in love with me." Now please don't think I'm Mrs. Wonderful, because I don't do that very often. But it's worth a try!

I remember a gift my dad gave my mom one Christmas.

16

He took fifty-two pieces of candy, unwrapped each one and placed a note inside with a promise to her. Then he re-wrapped them. One promise was for a dinner at a nice restaurant. Another was for a new dress. Then there were others that simply said, "I love you" or "Collect one big kiss." Not only did she have his love notes and promises to look forward to each week, but she had Christmas all year long. (I told them they needed a couple more kids and a cat.)

## The Giving of Unusual Compliments

"You can catch more flies with honey than with vinegar" — that's a frequently quoted saying. I know it's true. When I am out ministering, I make a point to remember every compliment that I hear about Randi, so that when I return home, I can tell him how much he is valued.

But remember, there is a difference between genuine compliments and flattery. "A lying tongue hateth those that are afflicted by it; and a flattering mouth worketh ruin" (Prov. 26:28).

I once attended a gathering where a young woman was working the room. She told the hostess her sparsely furnished, one-bedroom apartment was adorable. She told my friend the perm she had just gotten that morning was simply gorgeous (anyone with eyes could see that her hair resembled that of a really ugly poodle!). Then she got to me. She said, "Oh, Cathy, you have such a pretty face." To me, the interpretation of her comment was, "The rest of you is a hideous blob, but as a Christian, I feel obligated to say something nice."

A true compliment is like a salve to our soul. Take a few minutes to remember seven characteristics that first attracted you to your husband or drew you to a friend. Then, every day for a week tell that person one of those seven reasons why you cherish him. Let him know how knowing him has affected you. A sincere compliment is a tremendous gift.

## Give Them Some Space

Having time to spend with individual friends is essential for married couples. Encourage your spouse to spend time with his friends. And when you are with your friends, don't compare spouses.

Sometimes my husband will insist that the children leave me alone so I can fill the garden tub and have a restful bubble bath. This requires locking the door so I don't have five little ones, clothes and all, splashing around with mommy.

## Take a Drive Through the Country

I remember my father telling me about his grandfather, a farmer, who rode a horse-drawn wagon into town to sell his vegetables. "It took almost half a day," he said. My great grandfather had much time to reflect on things as he drove through the country.

I often wish life these days could be lived at a slower pace. Today, if we get annoyed at someone, all we have to do is pick up the phone and instantly tell them off, whether they are across the street or around the world. We just don't want to expend the time or energy to do what we know is right — for our spouses, our children or our friends.

I'm reminded of a beautiful, but sad, scripture from the Song of Solomon.

> "I am come into my garden, my sister, my spouse: I have gathered my myrrh with my spice; I have eaten my honeycomb with my honey; I have drunk my wine with my milk...it is the voice of my beloved that knocketh, saying, Open to me, my

sister, my love, my dove, my undefiled: for my
head is filled with dew." (Her answer) "I have put
off my coat; how shall I put it on? I have washed
my feet; how shall I defile them? I opened to my
beloved; but my beloved had withdrawn himself,
and was gone" (5:1-3,6).

What is the message here? She says, *I don't want to be
inconvenienced. I've taken off my robe and gone to bed. If I
get up to open the door, my feet will get dirty.*

How many relationships have we abandoned because the
time it took to develop and preserve them just didn't fit our
schedule? Paul tells us in Ephesians, "Redeeming the time,
because the days are evil" (5:16).

Do you remember years ago when a company issued
green stamps if we made purchases at certain stores? They
were just useless pieces of paper until we took them to the
store and redeemed them.

Each of us has just so much allotted time to redeem. I
urge you to use it on your most precious relationships.

# 2

# Marriage — the Sandpaper of the Holy Spirit

God created a woman out of Adam's rib and called her Eve. That's when the garden got interesting.

Adam and Eve had to be married, even though we never read about the ceremony. Maybe since there were just the two of them, it was hard to find a best man and bridesmaids. On top of that, who was there to come and cry and eat those funny little hot dogs wrapped in biscuit dough?

Adam and Eve had a lifetime — 930 years to be exact — of great joy and fellowship coupled with blame and shame, sorrow and pain. They suffered the loss of two sons, one to murder and the other to sin. Adam and Eve, like most married couples, discovered that married life isn't always a bowl of cherries. Sometimes it's the pits.

## How Can Something So Wonderful Hurt So Much?

Relationships can be the spice of life or the heartburn of the soul. Every truly successful man or woman knows that when all is said and done, it's not the money or honor or fame that comforts you. It is loving and being loved that fulfill the heart of a person.

God expressed His desire for union when He told Adam it was not good to dwell alone. To help maintain a state of union, God graciously gave principles and laws that apply to marriage. He told the husband to love his wife as Christ loved the church. He instructed the wife to obey, yield and submit to her husband (Eph. 5:22,25).

## Get With the Program, Baby

Let us imagine that one of the marriage partners does not follow God's guidelines for a successful and joyous marriage. Of course, this would never really happen, but we will assume it just for discussion purposes.

This is the neat part of God's plan for us. He took into account that no matter how hard we may try to succeed, we occasionally blow it. God foresaw the imperfections of those He created and loves so much, and He provided the perfect redemption plan. That plan releases us from our natural tendency to turn inward with hopelessness and self-pity.

Do not give up on your marriage. I prophesy to you in the name of our Lord Jesus and by His Holy Spirit that God has already provided what you need for a successful marriage. Your marriage can be all the things you desire it to be.

My own marriage is a testimony of God's ability to take two wounded, shattered and disappointed hearts and heal them. When we were at our lowest point, we did not even want to try to make it work. Vows were broken, trust destroyed and lives left in ruin.

Just when I needed them most, God gave me some scriptural principles and simple promises that saved my marriage, and I would like to encourage you with them.

## Pardon Me, but Can You Spare a Sheep?

The Lord used Abigail to teach all women a valuable lesson on living and dealing with a difficult and angry man. She had to cope, and she did so successfully. Let me give you some background information on this remarkable woman.

The story of Abigail is found in 1 Samuel 25. In the preceding chapters of this book the Bible indicates that Saul had rewarded David with a job at his palace after David slew Goliath. Saul made David his full-time minister of music.

Saul loved the favor of God and the gift of God that David brought with him to the palace. Yet, at the same time he hated it. Saul even tried to kill David, because he rejected the new anointing that David had.

The new anointing, typified by David's gift, causes people to sing new praises, which causes older ministries to be tempted to be jealous. But all that needs to be done in the kingdom cannot be accomplished by one type of ministry.

David ran for his life from Saul's wrath and holed up in a cave near the city of Gath. When the word spread about where David was, four hundred distraught, dissatisfied, unhappy debtors showed up at his cave for dinner. This number did not include the family members who came. David had a cave full of refugees.

David moved his men to Carmel, and that became his guerrilla territory. In the middle of this territory were sheep that belonged to a man by the name of Nabal. David now had six hundred men to feed, and there was no doubt a great temptation to snatch a sheep or two. Instead, David and his men provided a wall of protection around Nabal's servants.

It was sheep-shearing time, which was also party time in Carmel. David got wind of it and sent ten young men to Nabal's house. Considering the protection he had provided to Nabal's property, David felt he could ask Nabal for some food for his men.

Nabal made a grave mistake. "Who is David, and why would I take my food and give it to him?" he responded (see 1 Sam. 25:10-11). Everyone knew who David was, including Nabal's household.

When David's men returned and reported Nabal's refusal, David became enraged. He told his men, "Put on your swords."

## Abigail — You Gotta Love Her

Nabal's servants were appalled. Their master had just sentenced them to disaster. David vowed that not one male among Nabal's household would still be alive the following morning.

The servants ran for help — not to Nabal, but to his wife, Abigail. She quickly assembled a banquet for six hundred. The Word tells us that she grabbed, among other things, two hundred loaves of bread. That would require one gigantic oven!

I think of my microwave oven, which doubles as a very expensive bread box when it's not in use. I have stuffed a lot of things in there, including English muffins, plastic bags of leftover, burnt-bottom biscuits from the previous week and three fruit cakes that my husband purchased — one for each of the last three Christmases.

Abigail sent the food and the servants ahead of her. When she saw David, she threw herself on the ground at his feet and began doing some fast talking. David was completely won over by this woman's humility and generosity, and he spared her household. She returned home to find her husband drunk, so she didn't say a word about what she had done until morning.

## Beauty and the Beast

The name *Nabal* literally means "a fool." He was a descendant of the very spiritual house of Caleb, and he should have known better. It's far worse when a person knows all the religious jargon and chooses not to do right.

Nabal was very great and very rich. But the Revised Standard Version of the Bible calls Nabal churlish. That is an old English word that means surly, boorish and miserly. He was not pleasant to work with. This man was evil in his doings; he had a drinking problem; he was rude and selfish; and he railed at the servants of David.

Abigail was everything her husband was not. She was a woman of good understanding, intelligence and breeding. She was beautiful and approachable; the servants respected her. This woman had courage and knew how to deal tactfully with people, especially her husband. She possessed "tongue control." She waited until the proper time to tell Nabal what had happened.

Here are two totally incompatible people, stuck in a relationship. How did Abigail live with this man? How did she ever get entangled with him anyway? Maybe he won her in the wife lottery after buying all the tickets.

She managed to live with Nabal because she had a three-pronged commitment: to her Maker, her marriage and her mate.

## Committed to Her Maker

Listen to the principles of faith Abigail declared in her speech to David (see 1 Sam. 25:26-31):

*The Lord lives*...therefore He has power to uphold righteousness for me.

*The Lord avenges*...I do not need to judge Nabal, because the Lord will do that.

*The Lord sets up who He wills*...that means He set up Nabal and chose me to be his wife. It also means that I am at the right place, even though it is not a very nice place right now.

*The Lord loves holy people*...therefore my job is to stay holy no matter what Nabal is like.

Abigail had the right perspective. "The Lord can cope with His enemies because the Lord is good."

These truths must have been difficult for her to believe at times. Can you imagine what it must have been like for her? It certainly must have looked totally hopeless in the natural. But Abigail was committed to the Lord her God, and she knew David would be blessed because he, too, was committed to God.

## Committed to Her Marriage

You can never be committed to your marriage if you are looking for an "out" all the time, living with one foot out the door of your marriage commitment. There are things that drive you crazy about your spouse, but they are not grounds for divorce. Abigail was looking for ways to make her marriage work and found them. She wasn't looking for excuses to bail out. She believed that marriage was God's way...forever.

## Committed to Her Mate

I know Abigail was committed to Nabal, because she didn't look to David for compensation after she served food to his men. She did not look for the opportunity to cheat on Nabal, even though he was hard to love. I don't know what their sex life was like; I do know he was drunk a lot. Abigail couldn't help but notice what a handsome, kind, godly man David was.

David had an eye for a pretty girl. As soon as Nabal was out of the way (I'll tell you later how that happened), David went after Abigail so fast she didn't have time to go to Victoria's Secret for a trousseau. However, anyone that can whip up a dinner for six hundred should be prepared for almost anything.'

Out there in the desert, Abigail had every opportunity to use her charms just as Bathsheba did. But she didn't, because she was committed to Nabal even though he was a sorry excuse for a man. It would have been very easy to offer herself to David as a present. She could have compromised and walked off with him while Nabal was still alive, but she didn't choose that path.

David did not try to seduce her. I believe he sensed the quality of this woman and knew she was committed. Some of us would have been so angry we would have drawn David a map to Nabal's room and told him to go get him. But Abigail had no malice in her heart. She risked her life to save Nabal, so deep was her commitment to him.

## We Just Aren't Compatible

Sometimes marriage involves two incompatible people, and by the power of God they iron out their differences. Now that's an adventure in marriage...an Abigail and a Nabal.

When my husband and I got married, we knew some changes were going to be made, but we each thought the other would do the changing. The goal was getting my partner to do it *my* way, which was obviously much better than *his* way.

Abigail did not try to change Nabal. Nor did she close her eyes to the facts. Love sees. Contrary to popular thinking, love is not blind. What Abigail did was extraordinary. She took the whole situation upon herself. She told David, "I did not see your servants. I must be responsible in some way" (see 1 Sam. 25:25).

If you live with a difficult man or woman, consider your efforts in relating to him or her as practice for dealing with difficult people outside your home. Thank God for the experience and the fact that He can trust you with it. Abigail had a lot of practice in dealing with Nabal, so when the situation with David came along she knew exactly what the Lord expected her to do.

## Principles I Learned From Abigail

*Abigail agreed with her adversary.* If you retaliate in anger, the door for the spirit of strife will be opened. The next time your spouse is angry and you want to yell out with hateful words, find something to agree on instead.

*Abigail asked for forgiveness.* Find something to be sorry about. It may take creative thinking. Be willing to say you are sorry even when everything within you is screaming out, "What do I have to be sorry about?"

*Abigail gave her advice.* Unless you can find something to be sorry about, don't offer your advice. Abigail was watching like a hawk for her opportunity to approach David. She went directly to his relationship with his Lord. She prophesied his future, telling him that the Lord was setting him up to be king. She reminded him how much the Lord loved him. She went right to his heart, and it worked.

*Abigail decided to serve Nabal.* She was there to meet her husband's needs even though she recognized that he was not there to meet hers. She was a servant, and that was a challenge in itself. We have lost that concept in these days. Where is there a better place to serve than in a marriage? If you serve your spouse during a difficult situation, don't be surprised if you see a positive change.

*Abigail possessed the tongue of the wise scribe.* She knew when to speak and when to keep silent, and her self-control saved her life. Many times we vow never to bring up a touchy subject again, but we continually break our vow. When they come through the door, we let them have it.

Abigail had just saved her husband's life, yet she didn't let him know it. If I had been she, I would have announced it on the six o'clock news. She realized he was drunk and wouldn't hear what she said anyway, so she put him to bed.

We don't read how she did it, but when she told him all that she had done, he had a heart attack. (That's the truth — see 1 Sam. 25:37.) Ten days later Nabal was dead.

*Abigail demonstrated remarkable courage.* I guess she figured she had nothing to lose. She risked everything, not knowing what the result would be. We need to fight for our spouse until the end, just as Abigail did. Risk everything and do something, even if your spouse will not. The Lord will bless you for it.

## Take My Nabal, Please!

The moral of this story is *not* "Do the right thing, and God will kill your husband and give you a King David."

This account of Abigail, Nabal and David is about hope. It shows that it is possible to live with a difficult person and cope with angry people. It challenges us, with the help of God's Spirit, to see a picture of God's love.

I'm astounded to see as many women as I do in miserable marriages today. They go from one miserable marriage right into another. Gradually, their feelings of loss and hopelessness give way to either despair or apathy. There is no situation quite as desperate as having no hope for a marriage or any other kind of union, including ministry, work and family relationships.

Unlike marriages in America, marriages in Abigail's day were arranged. By law, she was in a relationship that gave her financial security. But it robbed her of self-esteem.

Abigail could have remained in her marriage by one of two means: 1) by exercising sheer will power because she had no choice but to endure it; or 2) by remaining steadfast in her love for God.

Abigail did not know the end of her story when she married Nabal. As she arose each morning to attend to her tasks, one of which was serving a selfish husband she did not know that her deliverance was right around the corner. Neither did she realize that she would one day become the wife of the king of Israel.

We do know two things for sure: She knew God, and she knew the Word of God. One of my favorite Scriptures could very well have been hers: "Know therefore that the Lord thy God, he is God, the faithful God, which keepeth covenant and mercy with them that love him and keep his commandments to a thousand generations" (Deut. 7:9).

You see, her trust was *not* in her husband or in her marriage. Her trust and confidence was in God. That is why she ministered to David and his men in spite of hostility from Nabal. That is also why she could face David in his murderous rage. She trusted in the Lord. I believe that she also forgave and forgave and forgave. Her obedience and trust brought her deliverance.

In Abigail we see a strength and a dignity beyond natural capability. She knew *what* God could do even if she did know *how* He would do it.

It was my trust in God's unfailing love that brought a glimmer of hope in the darkest hour of my own failing marriage. It was a small, microscopic, infinitesimal glimmer, but it was there. It was the rope thrown out to me when I was drowning, a cord of God's love that assured me He was bringing us through, and that one day I would laugh and love again.

Truly, my marriage is a testimony of His grace!

# 3

# Job's Wife — the Dripping Faucet

**M**y husband and I were in a fruit market when we overheard a conversation between an elderly couple that went something like this:

"Mona, I want some peaches. Get me some peaches."

"Harry, you don't like peaches."

"Yes I do, Mona. I've been eating peaches for seventy-five years, and today I want some peaches."

"You don't like peaches; they give you gas. You are not getting any peaches. Get in the car. We're going home."

My husband, Randi, felt so sorry for Harry he was ready to buy a couple of peaches for him, one for Harry to eat and one for Harry to throw at Mona.

For years thereafter, whenever I tried to help my husband with my excellent counsel — which I believed was far better than any idea he could possibly have — all he had to do was look at me and say, "I like peaches, Mona."

Eventually it got so that all he had to do was turn to me and say "peaches," and I would see myself in that market with "Mona" written all over me. Sometimes when we had company over, Randi would use our secret "peaches" password. People wondered why I would suddenly drop the subject and get quiet, for a while at least. They wondered if it was a subliminal message that he used to silence me.

Solomon wrote these words:

> A quarrelsome wife is like a constant dripping on a rainy day; restraining her is like restraining the wind or grasping oil with the hand (Prov. 27:15-16, NIV).

Solomon was a man who knew women. After all, didn't he have seven hundred wives and three hundred concubines? There were hormones flying all around his palace. I am certain he knew what he was talking about when he wrote those verses.

We all have heard about the suffering of Job. In just a short time, this man went from living a life of luxury to lying on a bed of ashes. But what about his wife? Everything that happened to Job also happened to her.

Everything was going great. Then, the Word says, "There was a day..." (Job 2:1).

There was a day in the life of Job's wife, the dripping faucet, when her world fell apart. Job may have lived in fear for a long time, the fear that one day something awful was going to happen. Some terrible thing is going to touch my family, my finances — one day it will happen.

We live in a society in which many live in fear that something will come along to rob them of their finances, family and security. It is sad, but the truth is that the more we possess, the more we have to worry about.

Job was the most famous man in all the region. The New

31

International Version says his "path was drenched with cream" (Job 29:6). It seems his steps were bathed with butter. He was an oil man — olive oil, that is, and he was very wealthy. He was upright and spiritually mature, faithfully instructing his children in the ways of God. Then one day Satan came to accuse him.

Who is Satan, and why would he even care about us? We are told in the Word that he is a nasty fellow. God calls him the accuser of the brethren, a serpent, the devil, the morning star (Lucifer), father of lies, our adversary, the prince and the power of the air. He was the minister of music in heaven and had great authority until he said, "I *will* be greater than God one day" and got kicked out of heaven.

Satan was never the Creator; he was created. He hates God and people, especially the righteous.

He went after Job and his family. In Job 1:7 God asks Satan where he has been. Satan has access to God's throne because that is where he does all of his accusing. God knew that Satan had been out sniffing around Job's hedge of protection. Knowing this, God asked, "Have you considered my servant Job?" (Job 1:8, RSV).

"Of course he's good," the devil answered. "Of course he loves You. You have always protected and kept him. Just let him suffer a little, and see how he acts" (see Job 1:9-11).

Our loving God does not need a demonstration of His servants' integrity to silence some doubt in His mind. God knew exactly what was going to happen. God knows things that Satan doesn't, and He knew the end of the book of Job. So Job's test really put Satan in his place (under our feet, of course). God allowed Satan to "do his thing" so He could demonstrate to him that Job was His faithful servant.

The enemy makes a lot of mistakes. He persecuted the early church, and he crucified Jesus. He really must have been angry when Jesus walked out of that burial cave.

What made Job so extraordinary was the way he suffered.

32

His reaction during his suffering was incredible. However, I identify more with Job's wife.

I have a tendency to whimper a lot when I suffer. I also like to have as many people as possible know that I am suffering. I need to eat Little Debbie cakes to help me through my suffering. I hate it, and I am terrible at it. That's why I hate going to the dentist, pantyhose that are far too short and getting my hair pulled through the frosting cap with that torturous little crochet hook. If I had lived during the first century, I might even have been one of those Christians who stayed home and watched my television pastor entertain a lion or two while my friends were being eaten by them.

## Why Do They Call It an Act of God?

Job 2:7 tells us that Satan smote Job. *Smote* — that's an old English word that means: "smacked him up the side of the head and made sure that the only thing Job had left was a faintly beating heart."

What did our little dripping tap do? Did she go to the ash heap and comfort her husband? Did she hold him in her arms and lovingly remind him that for better or worse, richer or poorer, in sickness and in health until death parted them, they would come through this thing together? At the very least, she could have tenderly put her arms around him and said, "Come on home, old man, I'll put you to bed."

Now let's be fair. The ten children they lost were her children too. Her possessions were taken, her servants were gone and her husband was stricken. Her reputation was crushed. It was a devastating situation, and she had plenty to drip about.

But you don't start dripping when troubles come; you start dripping years before. It becomes a habit.

## Your Room Looks Like a Pigpen;
## Do I Look Like Your Personal Maid?

Job's wife bore ten children for Job. That in itself would have given her a lifetime of stuff to drip about. I have six children, and on some days if you were to come to my house you would find me dressed in the same muumuu I've had on for three days, sitting in a chair with a glazed look on my face.

When I had only one child, my house was always immaculate. No dishes in the sink, no moldy Jell-O and marshmallow stuff in the fridge, forgotten since last Thanksgiving. Now that our family has expanded to include five young children, my house resembles...well, it doesn't resemble my former immaculate home.

Even though Job's wife had ten children, a big house and plenty of servants, I tend to believe all these weren't enough for her. If she was like most of us, she probably complained about the children's dirty feet and messy rooms and the continual racket they made. When you are a dripping tap, there will always be something to complain about.

As I said, your dripping doesn't begin when the trouble comes. It is a habit that starts years before. I can just imagine Job's wife standing over his bed of ashes, hands on her hips, glaring down at him. If Job had the strength, I think he would have screamed! He probably wondered, *Why didn't I turn off her tap years ago?*

When someone is a complainer, he or she is never content. I wonder if all the material possessions and wealth Job provided for his wife actually made her happy. If he had seven thousand sheep, why not seven thousand rams, one for each sheep? It probably didn't matter if she had a beautiful home as long as her children didn't have better ones. She probably dripped about all the extra work her husband made for her when he brought home company for dinner (sound familiar?).

Job really did love his wife. He didn't want anyone else but her! He said, "I have made a covenant with my eyes not to look upon a maiden" (see Job 31:1). She was secure in his love. She had it made. Yet trouble came, and the tap opened up and became a torrent.

Why did Satan spare Job's wife? Everything and everyone else was taken from him, yet his wife was allowed to live. Satan knew he could use her to destroy Job's faith. God forbid that any of us would be allowed to live in order to discourage others and destroy their faith and their trust in God.

## Hearing But Not Believing

I was recently in a series of meetings that, according to all involved, were very successful. The anointing of the Lord was so sweet, the prophetic word was accurate, and many lives were changed, encouraged and given clear direction.

I was elated as we drove home. Then I reached into my pocket and retrieved an envelope that was handed to me after one of the meetings. It was a tithing envelope! Great! I was sure someone had given me a large offering and wanted to be sure I received it personally. My excitement soon evaporated when I opened it, only to find a note which I read in astonishment. It was one of those notes "written in love" to help me in my ministry. It was full of criticism and anger. It read something like, "Cathy, I just wanted to ask your forgiveness for thinking that you are a total dweeb, and I really do not think that you are as 'hot' as everyone says you are. In fact, not only was I disappointed in your ministry, but I believe my 'gopher' could minister better than you. I hope that this note has encouraged you and that you will accept my apology for being inattentive while you were speaking, as I found you extremely boring."

Then she asked me to forgive her for feeling the way she did. And to top it all off, she did not have the courtesy to sign her name so I would know who to order the hit for.

Deflated would be a mild description of how I felt after reading those words of discouragement. I have since destroyed the note, which accounts for the fact that I have to rely on my memory for the contents.

Do you know what reflecting on the note caused me to do? I gave power to the enemy to use those words to take out of my heart all the joy that had overflowed only moments before.

When I asked the Lord if any of what she said was true, He reminded me of the Scripture that tells us to beware when all men speak well of us. He also caused me to remember the times when I had let the enemy use my tongue to wound my husband, my daughter or a friend.

The words we speak (or write) are very important, especially when they can throw a lifeline to someone who is struggling. A misplaced word can cause a wound that will destroy the confidence of a precious child of God. Confidence that took a long time to build can then require months to restore.

Job's wife could have been a woman like the one described in Proverbs 31. But what did she do with her position? Instead of being the proverbial wife, she did nothing. From what I have read about her, I am of the opinion that she did not use her home, her position or her wealth to help others.

It was her husband who did that. Job stretched out his hands to the poor, helped the fatherless, caused the widow's heart to sing, worked among the blind and the lame and judged the wicked (see Job 29:12-17).

I think Job's gift of mercy spoiled his wife. She never came close enough to other people's suffering, so when the time came for her to provide comfort, she was totally unprepared.

When you live in abundance, there is always a temptation not to get involved in other people's sufferings. Job's wife lived in a world focused on *her* problems, *her* children, *her* husband. When all these were taken from her, she was left devastated. Her bitterness overflowed. Her anger erupted.

Suffering does not *create* your spirit; it *reveals* your spirit.

Out of the abundance of the heart, the mouth speaks. In other words, what moves the heart wags the tongue. There is something about the hard places that causes us to look into our own hearts.

The substance you are filled with is what drips along the way and becomes a torrent that erupts during suffering. Remember, a cup that is filled with sweet water cannot spill out one bitter drop.

## Good-bye Old Boy — It Was Nice While It Lasted

When you have nothing to drip about — *don't!* I have never heard so many people complain about such minor things as I do today. We complain about the house, the car, the kids, the church. Praise God that you have a house instead of a refugee tent. Thank God that you have a strong, smart little child who can talk and walk. Many aren't as blessed.

Ask those in your home — people with whom you are in daily contact — "Am I a grumbler and complainer? Do I show my appreciation and my gratitude enough to you? If I am a grumbler, please stop me. Help me to break the cycle. I'm sorry if I have been driving you crazy with my nagging."

Most men (or women) give in to their spouse's demands because there is hell to pay if they do not go along with all the complaining. They agree just to avoid an argument. Often, they withdraw. But the absence of war is not necessarily peace!

## Are You a Weeping Willow or a Cedar of Lebanon?

Many times when I have been in a hard place I have asked, "What kind of God are You to allow this to happen?" Total trust was not the key element in my suffering. I wanted answers.

Suffering will turn you either toward God or away from Him. Affliction caused Job's wife to curse God, but it caused Job to bless Him! It's either one or the other.

The great temptation during times of affliction is to take off with your husband's Visa card and head to Tahiti. I'm sorry, I didn't mean Tahiti — I meant the Caribbean.

A greater temptation is to blame someone else for the impossible circumstances that you must face. Job's wife blamed her husband. She could have been a great comfort to him in his time of sorrow. Instead, she was consumed with her own self-pity.

I'm reminded of Jesus when His hour of suffering came upon Him. He thought of His mother Mary and John, his best friend. Even in His agony, He remembered a total stranger — the thief on the cross, the one who really deserved his punishment. Jesus thought of the soldiers and of Simeon from Cyrene: "I'm asking you only to carry My cross. I am willing to die on it for you."

Jesus responded to suffering by reaching out to those in need. Our little dripping tap, Job's wife, thought only of herself. She was totally selfish.

I wonder if Job's wife ever wished for a second chance. Do you think she had pangs of guilt? When her husband's name was mentioned in the market, do you think a small pain stabbed at her heart? I wonder, after the immediate shock and grief began to wear off, if she ever cried out, "If only I had another chance, I'd do it differently."

## Starting Over When I Thought I Was Finished

Now, I don't want to make Job look superhuman. After listening to his so-called friends yak about his problems, he got a little feisty. He described how he had lived a good life, and then he challenged God. "I sign now my defense — let the Almighty answer me" (Job 31:35, NIV).

Well, God explained things to Job, Job repented, and then God asked Job to pray for his drippy friends. Frankly, I think they needed a kick in the pants.

After Job prayed for his friends, the Lord made him prosperous again and gave him twice as much as he had before (see Job 42:10). Then all of Job's relatives showed up at his house — without being invited, I might add — and brought gifts with them.

> And the Lord blessed the latter days of Job more
> than his beginning (Job 42:12, RSV).

The Bible tells us that Job had seven more sons and three more daughters. Since it does not say that Job's wife died and God gave him a Bo Derek type as a new wife, we must assume that Job's wife returned to him and their love life resumed. She bore him ten more children, and she got the second chance she needed.

I believe these children had a different spirit. The Scriptures mention the daughters by name and declare their renowned beauty. Job gave his daughters an inheritance along with what he gave their brothers.

I wonder if Job's wife, having once lost it all, stopped her dripping and began to appreciate a husband who was full of integrity. Did she value her relationships, her marriage, her wealth and her position more now than she ever did before?

Her first set of children were spoiled party animals. "As is the mother, so is her daughter" (Ezek. 16:44). We know that

Job's second set of daughters were exceptional. I believe that this was a sign of a change in their mother.

Ezekiel 16:46 is a good verse to remember when your child throws a fit in public that makes you want to disappear. Does he or she have your spirit? Before you throw this book at me, let me remind you, there is always hope. Look at Job's wife!

## I'd Love to Bake Them Some Brownies

After moving into a larger home, I was busy putting together beds and getting the kitchen in order when I heard a commotion outside. I ran out the back door just in time to hear my neighbors cursing at one of my sons, who happened to be one centimeter over our boundary into their yard.

After retrieving my son, I walked over to apologize and introduce myself to them. It occurred to me that I had not been formally welcomed into the neighborhood. A few minutes later, I knew why. The couple informed me that they did not like us and that we were not welcome in the neighborhood. There was nothing I could possibly do or say to bring peace. I was stunned.

I realized that it would now become my task to try to get these people to love us.

One day in particular stands out in my mind. I "dressed" the boys to go out and play in the back yard. They wanted to wear hats, but I couldn't find any. Instead, my creativity rose up within me, and I took two pair of pantyhose, one for each boy, and put the panty part on their heads with the cotton crotch sticking up. Not knowing what to do with the legs, I thought they would make an excellent turban, so I wrapped them around their heads.

They really did look funny. We were having a good time and became rather boisterous. Suddenly, one of the boys broke loose and ran into our neighbor's open garage (that was before we put up our fence) with my poodle Bo in hot pursuit, barking one of those annoying "I'm going to wee-wee on your leg" barks. Knowing how much our neighbors already loved us, I grabbed all three — two boys and one dog — and ran for the protection of my house. Of course, that incident didn't help improve an already sick relationship with our neighbors.

Every time I saw the woman next door, I thought about Job's wife. This neighbor bore the look of bitterness. Her eyes were hard, and there was anger in every word she spoke. Bigotry and hatred seethed just below the surface.

I thought, *Wasted years, wasted life, and the joy of becoming friends and enjoying a wonderful relationship shot down before ever given a chance to blossom.*

I pray for them, though I hear they are planning to sell their house and move away. I wonder if they will ever wish that they had a second chance.

My friend, do not waste the precious living water that you carry within you. Don't waste it by becoming a dripping faucet, complaining and grumbling all through your life.

# 4

# Why Am I Always the One With Chipmunk Cheeks?

**W**hat a tremendous meeting! The Spirit of the Lord was so strong that I felt as though I were speaking as the very oracle of God. Praise and worship were so heavenly that we thought we were in the very throne room of the Almighty. The accuracy of the prophetic word was awesome.

No one wanted to leave at the end of the meeting, we all wanted to linger in the presence of the Holy Spirit. Some were weeping, some were still worshiping and others were laughing because they were filled to capacity with the joy of the Lord. Laying on the floor across the front of the altar, scores of believers appeared drunk as in Acts 2.

Noticing the line of people waiting for prayer, I made my way to them. After ministering to them I glanced at my watch and realized that I had been standing for over an hour, so I reached for my Bible and prepared to leave. Just then, the last woman in the line grabbed me around the neck with one of those death locks that really exuberant Christians use. She took me by surprise. My face began to turn crimson, and I couldn't breathe for lack of oxygen. When she finally released me, tears had begun to sting my eyes from the pain of her shoulder blade in my Adam's apple. I could have been imagining it, but for a few seconds I thought I was drifting down a dark tunnel towards a brilliant light. It turned out to be the church elders flashing the sanctuary lights because they wanted to go home.

"Wait a minute, Cathy, don't go yet. During the worship service and again while you were speaking, the Lord began to speak to me," she said.

My face was now on auto pilot. I was tired, I had just had a near-death experience, and I was forcing my face to smile.

"Yes, precious. What did the Lord say?" I asked as sincerely as I could.

"The Lord told me to tell you that you are fat."

Suddenly, I wasn't tired anymore. My face still wore a smile, but now the smile tightened, and I could feel my eyes begin to narrow. Maybe I had misunderstood her!

I began to size up this dear, dear child of God. I was tempted to ask her to please close her eyes, because God was going to touch her in such a dynamic way that she would feel as though she had been struck by a fist. Glory!

Realizing that this temptation was not from the Holy Spirit, I waited with anticipation to hear what her next words would be. This dear saint went on to tell me that while she was praying for me, the Lord told her to give me a little card with six green herbal tablets on it and tell me that if I would follow the directions, I would lose weight. "This card contains only three days' worth," I told her. Yes, she knew that. And for only $250 I could sign up in a new and exciting multilevel marketing program that would make

me not only thin but rich as well. (Of course, it would benefit the kingdom of God.)

## Did God Actually Say That?

There were two things I learned during my brief
encounter with that dear sister. Because I have a prophetic
ministry, I often start addressing the one I am speaking to
with these words: "For the Spirit of the Lord says..." Then I
go on to share an impression that the Lord gave me while I
was praying for him or her.

I began to realize how common it has become in some
Christian circles to say, "The Lord told me..." It is a wonderful thing to spend time in the presence of the Lord, listening
to His voice. But there is a danger in devaluing the word of
the Lord.

I have often been in services where, under the prompting
of the Holy Spirit, I have been led to share a word from the
Lord, and it was extremely moving.

For instance, a word to one woman went like this: "The
Lord says, 'My daughter, you are more precious to Me than
ten thousand pieces of silver or gold. I have seen the wounds
brought on by the words of rejection and intimidation, and
I desire to heal those hurts. For I am your God, and you are
My daughter. The years of barrenness and unfruitfulness are
over, and you have entered a year of jubilee!'"

Upon hearing the word of the Lord for this woman, the
congregation, who knew her personal life, went wild, clapping and rejoicing, weeping because of the accuracy of the
word. What I did not know was that this woman had lived
with an abusive, alcoholic husband for years, and she suffered in her emotions and her health because she was in
bondage to a cruel man. That is why what happened next is
so incredulous to me.

The woman looked up at me through dry eyes and said,

"That's not what I wanted to hear. I was hoping to hear something about my new business."

God had just spoken a word of love and tremendous deliverance to this woman, and it wasn't the word she desired.

There is such value in the words of the Lord. We cannot afford to take His words lightly. Neither are we at liberty to say, "The Lord told me to tell you" without knowing for certain that He really did speak.

In the Old Testament, when the kings or rulers would come to the prophets because they needed to hear from God, they would bring gifts, great gifts. They were not trying to buy a favor from the prophet. They were giving an outward sign of an inner attitude toward the value of one word from the Lord.

One king took gifts to a prophet just for a one-word answer to the question, Am I going to live or not?

What value do you place on the promises of God? I know with great confidence that when God speaks, you can count on His Words coming to pass!

I recently received a letter from a pastor's wife that caused my heart to rejoice. Four years ago while I was ministering in her church, I prayed for her and her husband. The Lord told her through a personal prophecy that she would have a son and a daughter. Within a year, she gave birth to a son. Two years later she suffered a devastating miscarriage. After that experience, she was afraid to become pregnant again. She said, "I did not know if I could face the tragedy of losing another baby." Still, she remembered the word of the Lord she had received.

It is so amazing to discover what the promise of the Lord will do to our spirit man. Everything within us will cry out, No! But the promise of God is still there reminding us to rise up one more time. The word of the Lord will pull on our grain of mustard-seed faith and tell us that He *will* fulfill His word to us if we will stretch our faith.

45

The young woman finished her letter by telling me that she did indeed get pregnant again but began to bleed several times during the pregnancy. Nevertheless, while lying in bed, faith began to rise up in her concerning the promise of the baby to come. God did fulfill His word, and a healthy, beautiful child was born. Praise God!

## I Don't Like Your Word

I'm not sure just what it is about me that attracts unsolicited counsel, rebukes or prophecy (weird and otherwise). I seem to draw people out of their shells, because they frequently say something like, "Now, I've never done this before but..." and then go on to tell me some strange bit of information. I do appreciate this occasionally, like the time a woman told me I preached nearly an entire sermon with my blouse unbuttoned. However, I did *not* appreciate the lady who tried to be funny when she said my dress was lovely and added, "Too bad they didn't have it in *your* size."

My grandmother, who is eighty-nine years old, has spoken into my life many times. I guess the Lord uses her because He knows I would not actually hurt an eighty-nine-year-old lady, especially my own grandmother. However, there have been a few occasions when I could easily have helped send her on home to glory before her time was up. Like the time she called me and told me that she had something to say to me, but that it was really hard to do. She said she begged the Lord to use someone else, but the Lord told her she needed to do it.

Instantly my palms began to sweat. I had one of those "Oh, dear God, now what?" sinking feelings you get in the pit of your stomach.

"The Lord told me to tell you that you are filled with pride, and unless you humble yourself He will never be able to use you the way He desires to," she said.

Gripping the telephone in my hand, my jaw tightening, I said all the correct religious things that I had been trained to say: "Thank you, Gammy, for obeying the Lord. I certainly want to please Him. If you see something in me that stops the flow, I really want to know."

What came out of my mouth and what was erupting from my heart were two different things. My heart said, "I am not proud. If I had a problem with pride, God Himself would tell me; He wouldn't send a little old woman. I have ministered to thousands across the United States and overseas who think I'm not so bad."

Still, her words kept ringing in my ears. "Unless you humble yourself..." Could it really be true that somehow I had begun to exalt myself? The very fact that I had to ask myself that question was a clear indication that pride had moved in to displace humility.

Pride is a deceptive spirit that creeps into our hearts. It can cripple minds and destroy relationships.

## Can You Believe That?

While watching television several years ago, I heard Nicky Cruz, who was once a drug addict, share the depths of sin and depravity that invaded one of the countries he had visited.

On one of the main streets, prostitutes sat inside storefront windows as men selected them through the glass enclosures. One of the most alarming facts he shared was that satanic worship was on the rise. Satan worshipers did not stand on pentagrams in dark rooms wearing black hoods and capes. They had a much more sophisticated form of worship. They taught their disciples that the highest form of satanic worship was the worship of self. I almost fell out of my recliner.

In Ezekiel 28:1-6 and 11-17 the prophet describes what

47

happened in heaven when Satan fell. We get a glimpse of Satan's character when Ezekiel quotes God as saying to Satan, "Your heart was proud because of your beauty..." (v. 17, RSV).

When I was young, my parents would often talk about how they were disciplined by their parents. My brothers and I would counter with a comment like, "That was in olden times" — meaning that those examples didn't apply today. We as Christians often read the Old Testament as if its examples of godliness and righteousness are ancient history that doesn't apply to modern, enlightened Christians at all. The apostle Paul tells us quite plainly, "Now all these things happened unto them for examples: and they are written for our admonition, upon whom the ends of the world are come" (1 Cor. 10:11). Warnings against allowing pride to rule and ruin us are just as valid today as they were when they were written by the Old Testament prophets.

Here's an example of how pride reveals itself today.

The college and career group from our church was enjoying a fourth of July picnic around the pool in our backyard. As everyone was talking and laughing, our attention was drawn to one of the young ladies in the group. She was very beautiful. You know the kind. Each man in the church believed that God had told him that she was his wife-to-be, while all the girls prayed she would be led to attend another church.

All day long she announced to anyone within earshot that she had been "so fat" but had just lost ten pounds. (Don't you just hate it when absolutely gorgeous, trim girls keep repeating how fat they are so everyone will tell them they aren't?) She had never been fat.

After listening to her false humility all day, even the admiring young men grew tired of hearing it. So the next time she announced that she had lost ten pounds one of the men said, "Gee, it's too bad you lost it all off your chest!"

I know his comment was not the Christian thing to say, but when I heard it I laughed so hard I swallowed a watermelon seed, which later emerged from my nose.

Can you imagine a spirit so powerful that it wooed angels to rebel against God and leave heaven? Before there was evil, before there was an accuser or a beast, the power of pride was so great it could seduce angels to leave a perfect God and a perfect heaven.

Pride is masked in this "me too" generation as a means of building one's character and self-image. Pride manifests itself as self-sufficiency, which has not only wrecked the world but has crept into the church as well.

## Thank You, Mother, I Can Do It Myself

God created us to receive from Him in sweet simplicity. We need to be submissive, simple, humble vessels. Our answer should always be, "Here I am, Lord; use me." As God uses us, we begin to acquire understanding and knowledge from the Word. We can become somebody and something wonderful in Christ.

When our oldest child was learning to drive, I would begin to lecture her before we ever got into the car. Finally, she would roll her eyes at me and give me that "don't embarrass me" look that only teenagers can give. I realized I was too cautious, but I knew the danger out there if she did not learn her lessons well. It is pride that keeps us declaring, "I know that already. Don't you think I know what to do?" instead of, "I really don't know it all, God. Have mercy on me, and help me to be a good pupil."

Even toddlers express their independence. They put on their clothes slowly, sometimes upside down and backwards. When I try to help our little ones, they pull back and tell me, "No, Mommy, I do it!"

I believe that behind every church division there is pride.

Behind every denominational split there is pride. Every person who has lost his anointing has done so because he failed to kill that seed of pride. Behind every missed calling that was caused by disobedience there was pride. Pride holds us back from fulfilling what God wants to do in our lives.

The problem in the body of Christ that really grieves the Holy Spirit is not drugs or scandalous meetings in a hotel or another obvious sin. It is the pride from which it all stems. God resists only one type of person: the proud (see 1 Pet. 5:5). He can work with everything but pride. The Bible does not say He resists the drunkard, the dope addict or people consumed by any other kind of sin. It says He resists the proud. The Word also says that God gives grace to the humble. That means that when pride comes in, we are cut off from the grace of God. We need His grace to help us when the tests come.

## I Really Blew It!

I was so thrilled when the call came from my publisher — I was to be a guest on *The 700 Club*. Great joy! Did it really matter that I got the invitation in a trade-off that went something like this?

**Publisher:** We will give you T. D. Jakes and Dr. Fuchsia Pickett, but you have to take Cathy Lechner.

**The 700 Club:** Cathy who?

**Publisher:** OK, OK. We'll throw in Stephen Strang and Iverna Tompkins.

**The 700 Club:** Whatever!

So there I was, sitting off-camera, waiting for Pat Robertson and Terry "Miss-Absolutely-Gorgeous-Even-With-the-Flu" Meeuwsen to bring me on stage for an interview. All of a sudden, I found myself on the platform in front of two hundred billion viewers worldwide; then tragedy struck.

Three weeks prior to my interview, I had undergone surgery. I wish I could tell you that I had handled the recovery gracefully, but the truth is I do not do pain well. My mother, who was caring for me, had already indicated that I was an extremely difficult patient. The only reasons she didn't quit were that I was her daughter and she loves me.

As long as I had pain medicine, I was OK. The minute it wore off I was in trouble.

One of the side effects of being on the particular pain medicine I was using is dry mouth. The medication I had taken the night before had left my mouth as dry as cotton. Sitting on the chair opposite the adorable Terry, I panicked as I realized my top lip had stuck to my upper gum, leaving my top teeth hanging out and making me look like a Jerry Lewis character. I could answer only in monosyllables. I eyed her coffee mug on the table. Could I? Should I? Would Kathie Lee drink Regis' coffee?

"I'm sorry, what was the question?" I asked.

I spent the entire fourteen minutes of the segment fixating on my teeth. The opportunity of a lifetime, the door through which to launch an international ministry, and my lip was stuck to my gums.

**Terry:** "Cathy, as a wife, mother and minister, what is the one message that you would like to communicate to the billions of rich people who might send you a lot of money today *if* your answer is good?"

**Cathy:** "RIBBERSCHULNISTA."

**Terry:** "Uh huh. Well, that is all the time we have today. Thank you."

Sometimes it seems the Lord allows us to walk into situations that will force out pride and give us the opportunity to take on humility.

## I Am So Proud to Be So Humble

Do you realize that pride will feed on anything, even on a gift from God? Pride will feed on the anointing, on the gifts and on great worship. I love worship, but I have been in meetings where the leadership and the congregation began to worship the worship. Was it powerful enough, loud enough, magnificent enough? Were the people stirred; was I stirred? Who is the worship for, anyway?

On the other hand, I have been to meetings in a humble home where there were no instruments and no one had an outstanding voice. Yet, when we began to softly worship, the presence of the Lord entered in with great power.

Pride can feed on answered prayer: When Susie prays, things happen. Pride can reveal itself through talent, revelations, dreams, knowledge of the Word and visions. It manifests itself in many ways.

## If You Would Do What I Am Doing

We love pride because it doesn't challenge us. It is humility that makes us uncomfortable. When I returned from my first missions trip, I got a firsthand look at how much religious pride was in me.

On my first Sunday back home, I found myself being critical of the church. The people here had air conditioning, but did they appreciate it? Oh no! Look at everyone glancing at their watches. The poor Filipinos didn't care how long you preached; they wanted all they could get of God and His Word. In fact, most of them didn't even own a watch. On and on I judged. From the padded pews to the short and tidy sermon, I judged.

Several years later the Lord reminded me of my attitude when a fellow who ministered to street people at a soup kitchen got up in church and started to rebuke everyone who was not involved in his ministry because *his* ministry was the true ministry of Jesus. The Holy Spirit spoke to me and said, "That was you." You see, pride can manifest itself even through God-given zeal.

Our problem today is not the New Age movement or who the president is or what his wife has to say. Our problem is that we are not low enough for God to lift us up!

Pride is not interested in getting things done for God. Pride wants to let others know what *we* did and how *much* we did. It is totally preoccupied with our image before others. We feel the need to let others know that God is using us just a little more than He's using someone else.

We need to learn to root for one another. I know the pain and frustration of watching others receive the answers to the same prayers that I have prayed and fought so hard for. We *must* rejoice with others when they are blessed, because it puts us in a position to receive blessing when our time comes. Paul exhorted the church in Corinth, "And whether one member suffer, all the members suffer with it; or one member be honoured, all the members rejoice with it" (1 Cor. 12:26).

Pastor Jim Cymbala of the Brooklyn Tabernacle Church in New York City once preached what I consider to be the greatest message on the spirit of pride that I've ever heard. He made an amazing statement: "Pride has the eternal hostility of God. God resists [pride] as a general in full battle array to bring you down." This was his interpretation of 1 Peter 5:5.

When God looks down and sees pride, He smells the scent that ruined heaven, a scent very displeasing to Him.

I can easily see the times in my own life that pride separated me from people I loved and ruined relationships that God had given to me. Perhaps if I had just been willing to say I'm sorry or try one more time to humble myself and change my opinions, a friendship could have been saved, an argument avoided or a situation resolved.

I remember well the afternoon I broke one of my own rules — that no matter how desperate or bored I was, I would never, never, ever watch a stupid talk show. I suppose it was the title that caught my attention: "My Mother's Husband Ate Her Uncle's Socks, and I Just Can't Forgive Him." I was naive enough to think that perhaps that's where all those missing socks went, so I watched. What a mess! Those people on TV were revealing their most intimate secrets as well as those of their "loved ones." I noticed that no one ever said, "I'm sorry. What can I do to make it right?" Of course, no one ever apologizes. Otherwise the show would last only thirty seconds.

## Humble Pie Isn't All That Bad — It Tastes Like Chicken

God gives grace to the humble. We know that grace is the unmerited favor of God, but we need to see it as the exchange we receive for our pride. Everything we need for life is contained in God's grace. As we humble ourselves, we will receive the grace that contains power, love, wisdom and the leading of God.

## Why Is My Line So Long?

Have you ever participated in a communion service in which the pastor asks everyone to break their bread into little pieces, go to someone that they have something against and share the bread with them? That can be a real eye-opener, can't it? I went to a service like that. When I opened my eyes, before me stood a line of women with smiles on their faces that said, "I've been waiting for an opportunity like this for a long time. Now I can tell her how and when she offended me."

Each woman told me how I had offended her and then gave me a piece of her bread. By the end of the communion service, I looked like a chipmunk. I didn't realize I could store so much bread in my mouth! I suggest that we switch to those stick-to-your-tongue-wafers. You can't break those little things into very many pieces.

Once again, my eighty-nine-year-old grandmother was right. I repented of having a heart and mind filled with pride. It was not the first time nor the last. (I also repented for insisting we buy my grandmother a pair of in-line skates!)

It's frightening when you look at Scripture and see the roll call of those who lost everything because of pride. Lucifer lost his exalted position in heaven, and Nebuchadnezzar lost his kingdom and ate grass like an animal. Moses, known for his outstanding humility, missed going into the promised land because of pride. The really frightening thing for me is that God does not turn His back on us when we are lifted up in pride; He *faces* us and *resists* us with His might. "Wherefore he saith, God resisteth the proud, but giveth grace unto the humble" (James 4:6). The question we have to answer is this: Do we want His grace, or do we want His opposition?

# 5

# The Confessions of a Pastor's Wife

Imagine that you've just had a wonderful time in your prayer closet. You finally found that hour you so desperately needed to close yourself in with God. You had a great time praising, worshiping and pouring out your heart to God until you felt that sweet release in your spirit.

Renewed and feeling refreshed and clean, you left your prayer closet and walked out into your backyard only to be confronted by your angry, nasty neighbor. The conversation goes something like this:

**You:** Good morning, Mrs. Snotfester.

**Mrs. Snotfester:** Don't you good morning me! Your dog pooped in my yard again.

**You:** I am terribly sorry.

**Mrs. Snotfester:** The next time your dog is out, I'm

going to feed him rat poison. Then I'll call the Humane Society to come and pick him up.

**You:** Please, Mrs. Snotfester, it won't happen aga...

**Mrs. Snotfester:** Then I'm going to get in my huge green '68 Impala and back up over that mangy dog while I'm waiting for them to come.

**You:** I said I was sorry. Please forgive me.

**Mrs. Snotfester:** In fact, I don't like your nasty little children either. I am going to feed them to my boa constrictor.

**You:** All right, Mrs. Snotfester, that's it. Father in heaven, please close Your eyes because this isn't going to be very pretty.

You pray as you pick up the rake lying nearby. There goes your peace and your joy. And there goes the head of Mrs. Snotfester! Do you have anyone in your life who is difficult to deal with? God knew you would. He said, "Bless your enemies; no cursing under your breath" (Rom. 12:14, MSG).

A frog has a wonderful advantage in life — he can eat everything that bugs him.

Just because someone rubs you the wrong way doesn't mean he or she is a difficult person. We all have days when we are difficult to get along with. However, someone who is consistently sneaky, hostile, negative and unresponsive to others' needs is a difficult person. That's the person you're probably thinking of right now.

As a teenager, I had a job that God used to rub and polish me. Of course, at the time I thought it was just a satanic plot to destroy me. Now I see how God in His mercy was working for me and in me.

My boss was a backslidden, cigarette-smoking woman who could make your blood freeze just by staring at you. I was not only a preacher's kid but also an outspoken Christian. I became a target of her anger. She was angry at God and at Christians because of her failed marriage and her rebellious kids.

This woman ridiculed me because of my values. She chose my coworker as her pet and gave her extra breaks and extended her lunch hour. I had never met anyone with such a mean streak. She was so unjust that she delighted when evil won and when wrong was victorious over right.

I remember coming home from work, crying and telling my father, "I'm quitting. I don't have to put up with this. That free ham they give me at Christmas just isn't worth it."

My father said to me, "Cathy, you have a good job. There are people like her everywhere you go."

"Can I quit, Daddy?"

"No!" And that was that. I was squealing, God was cutting, and my flesh was dying — and it seemed that my enemy was triumphing.

After two years at that same job I was astonished when suddenly and unexpectedly my boss asked me if I would come to her house one evening.

The only thing I could think of was Hansel and Gretel, the witch and the oven.

I had been fasting and praying for two weeks for this woman. For two weeks I slipped into the church on my lunch hour and cried out to the Lord for deliverance from this person and from my job. Now I found myself confronted with an opportunity to talk to her. I heard myself saying, "Yes," and got directions to her home.

You can be sure I prayed in the Spirit all the way to her house. I was surprised to find that her home was really quite pleasant. I half expected black curtains at the window and dead animals in cages.

After offering me a drink, which I respectfully refused, she began to pour her heart out to me. She talked and cried for hours. She even swore.

As I sat there listening and watching her weep, I couldn't believe the emotions that welled up inside of me. Pity turned into compassion as I sensed God's presence and His overwhelming love for this woman sitting in front of me. Suddenly she looked old and very lonely; bitterness has a way of aging people. As I remembered the two years of mental torture this woman had put me through, I realized what was wrong with her. She was hurting desperately.

Fumbling for the right words, I put my hand over hers and shared the love of God with her. Although she didn't say the sinner's prayer with me that night, she let me pray for her. I knew something was broken, not only in this lady, but also inside of me.

From that night on until I quit the job just before my wedding, she talked differently to me. In front of the others she still kept up the sham of disrespect and irreverence, but we both knew things had changed between us.

You see, difficult people seldom accept responsibility for their behavior. They rarely repent, ask forgiveness or apologize.

> Don't hit back; discover beauty in everyone. If you've got it in you, get along with everybody. Don't insist on getting even; that's not for you to do. "I'll do the judging," says God. "I'll take care of it" (Rom. 12:17-19, MSG).

## You Wild Thing

> Don't be in any rush to become a teacher, my friends. Teaching is highly responsible work. Teachers are held to the strictest standards. And none of us are perfectly qualified. We get it wrong nearly every time we open our mouths. If you could find someone whose speech was perfectly true, you'd have a perfect person, in perfect control of life (James 3:1-3, MSG).

How many times have we spoken and then wished we could take back the words? It is the words we speak thoughtlessly but intentionally that cause us so much trouble.

The Word tells us that whatever is in our hearts will be spoken out of our mouths (see Matt. 12:34). That means that our hearts and our mouths are inextricably connected. Get the heart right, and the mouth will follow.

Why talk about the tongue in a book on relationships?

> A bit in the mouth of a horse controls the whole horse. A small rudder on a huge ship in the hands of a skilled captain sets a course in the face of the strongest winds. A word out of your mouth may seem of no account, but it can accomplish nearly anything — or destroy it!
>
> It only takes a spark, remember, to set off a forest fire. A careless or wrongly placed word out of your mouth can do that. By our speech we can ruin the world, turn harmony into chaos, throw mud on a reputation, send the whole world up in smoke and go up in smoke with it, smoke right from the pit of hell (James 3:3-6, MSG).

As pastors, Randi and I have made many lifelong friends. But we have also made our share of enemies. I was always comforted by the verse that tells us to beware when *everyone* speaks well of us. We *never* had that problem when we were pastoring a church.

A small group of our members got together to pray for the church and the staff. Wonderful things began to happen during the services as a result. People were saved, marriages were healed, and we felt the presence of God in every service.

Two of the ladies from this group began staying after the prayer meetings were over. They said they wanted to do some extensive, specialized prayer. Great! We could always use more prayer. One of the women was a brand-new

Christian and the other (I found out too late) had been invited to leave her last church because she had been stirring up trouble.

It wasn't long before they both became distant toward me. We found out later that they had begun to hold special prayer meetings in the home of the new convert, and many of our people were attending.

Suddenly, these two ladies and their families quit the church, taking two more families with them. When contacted and pressed for a reason, they replied very mysteriously, "The Lord will show you." (They rolled the rrrrrr so as to make themselves sound more spiritual!)

That is what they said to *us*. What they were saying to everyone else was a story about me that was so vile and sordid that I would be ashamed to put it in print. I was crushed and humiliated. When asked where they had received their information, they replied, "We got it all in the spirit." Just *whose* spirit they were talking about, they didn't realize.

About two years later I was teaching on offenses at a conference when I shared this story. I started weeping as I shared about words and their power to destroy.

After the altar service, I was surprised to see one of the women I was talking about, the new believer, waiting to talk to me. A friend had invited her to this conference, and she had accepted at the last minute not knowing that I was the main speaker. When she recognized me, she nearly fainted. As I spoke about the words and lies that had been used to try to destroy me, she realized the damage that had been done.

When I first saw her, I had a sick feeling in the pit of my stomach. She saw the apprehension on my face, and through sobs she said over and over that she was sorry.

She began to tell me what I already knew in my heart. The discontented families had tried to start a home church group. After only two months, they began to "bite and devour one another" (Gal. 5:15).

As we held each other our tears mingled, and God restored two hearts that night.

This illustration has a wonderful ending, except for the fact that those words released as truth did an enormous amount of damage. Repenting, saying she was sorry and seeking forgiveness was a great step toward the woman's restoration. However, her damaging words could never be retrieved.

> People who shrug off deliberate deceptions, saying, "I didn't mean it, I was only joking," Are worse than careless campers who walk away from smoldering campfires (Prov. 26:18-19, MSG).

When your heart is filled with the wisdom of the Word, you have a much better chance of releasing the wisdom of God when you open your mouth to speak.

The words of the Lord are like a hidden treasure. As we seek the Word of the Lord, God will allow it to be tried in our life in the furnace of testing until it is refined seven times.

Seven is the number of completion. God will cause the Word to be tried in our lives completely, and then it will be a part of us forever.

## Three Sources of Words

All words come from one of these places:

### 1. Realm of darkness

These words will first come as thoughts. They are real and loud. Do not listen to them. They are words of gloom, failure, despair, sickness, trouble, fear and misery. They speak of unhappiness, selfishness and unbelief.

## 2. Realm of light

These are God's words, Holy Ghost words. They speak of peace, joy, victory and health. They are encouraging words of prosperity, courage and blessing.

## 3. You

I love the story of little David as he stood before the giant Goliath. He stood there prophesying to the giant about what he and God were going to do to him. In my opinion, that giant was dead before the first stone was thrown. That's how great the power of words spoken in faith are.

> And I say to you, that every careless word that men shall speak, they shall render account for it in the day of judgment. For by your words you shall be justified, and by your words you shall be condemned (Matt. 12:36-37, NAS).

Words spoken from the realm of darkness also have power. For example: Do you find yourself falling into the trap of quarreling and bickering with your mate? Top that off with the silent treatment toward each other, and you have created a giant with your words.

What's your giant? It won't be killed with swords and spears. Start confessing that the Lord will help. He is faithful, and He will not fail.

Let the *sick* say: "With his stripes we are healed" (Is. 53:5).

Let the *fearful* say: "Yea, though I walk through the valley of the shadow of death, I will fear no evil: for thou art with me" (Ps. 23:4).

Let those in *battle* say: "If God be for us, who can be against us?" (Rom. 8:31).

Let those who *need strength* say: "The Lord is my strength

and my shield. My heart trusts in Him, and I am helped"
(Ps. 28:7, NIV).

Let the *discouraged* say: "He will never leave me nor for-
sake me. The Lord is my helper and I will not fear what
man may do to me" (see Heb. 13:5-6).

## Words

I want to share with you some special words from the
Scriptures.

The most beautiful word, *forgiveness*. "But with you there
is forgiveness; therefore you are feared" (Ps. 130:4, NIV).
Think how Peter must have felt to realize he had been forgiven after his denial of Jesus, or how the prodigal felt
upon receiving forgiveness from his father, or how you felt
the day it first dawned on you that you were forgiven.

The word that never comes back, *now*. "Behold, now is
the acceptable time; behold, now is the day of salvation" (2
Cor. 6:2, RSV). Even ten minutes ago is in the past, and ten
minutes from now is in the future. The only time we actually have is in the present.

God's favorite word, *come*. "The Spirit and the bride say,
'Come!'" (Rev. 22:17, NIV). This is the sweetest invitation
we will ever receive.

The hardest word, *no*. "'Let it be known to you, O king,
that we are not going to serve your gods nor worship the
golden image that you have set up'" (Dan. 3:18, NAS). *No* is
often the most difficult but the most rewarding word in the
long run. It's not for the "go along or get along" folks.

The meanest word, *whisper*. "A perverse man spreads
strife, and a whisperer separates close friends" (Prov. 16:28,
RSV). Years ago I read a story about a woman who had
sown malicious, untrue gossip about her pastor. Repentant,
she went to him and asked for his forgiveness. He said he
would, of course, forgive her and asked if she would do

one thing for him. "Anything," she said.

He took a feather pillow and walked to a nearby hill, opened it and let the wind take the feathers up, scattering them for miles. "Now," said the pastor, "go and gather up every last feather and bring it to me."

"But that is impossible," she stammered.

"Yes," he replied, "just as the words you spoke against me, even though you are sorry now, can never be retrieved or forgotten."

The weakest word, *if*. "He [the Lord] replied, 'If you have faith as small as a mustard seed, you can say to this mulberry tree, "Be uprooted and planted in the sea," and it will obey you'" (Luke 17:6, NIV). The disciples were saying that if they had more faith, they could do great things. Jesus told them they didn't need any more faith, they just needed to use what they had. We often say, "If things were different," or "If circumstances were changed." *If* becomes the biggest word in our vocabulary and cancels out our faith.

The word that moves God, *prayer*. "The prayer of a person living right with God is something powerful to be reckoned with" (James 5:16, MSG). What a promise! We all long for certain people or things to change — or for the power to change them — and yet God has given us the tool to make change happen.

Many times, I've had to take a close look at the words in my life. Were they words that move God? Or were they words from the realm of darkness, building up giants to destroy me?

Let me challenge you to do something that could be life-changing. Lay aside this book. With pen and paper, make three word lists. Head the first one *Negative Words*, the second *Positive Words* and the third *Challenging Words*. Pray and ask the Holy Spirit to show you the words you use that harm yourself and others. Make it a point to avoid those words and daily use the words that are positive and challenging — words that build up. Remember what Jesus said: "But those things which proceed out of the mouth come forth from the heart; and they defile the man" (Matt. 15:18).

If you are serious about going on to the next level with the Lord, start watching your words. Let this prayer of the psalmist be yours: "Let the words of my mouth, and the meditation of my heart, be acceptable in thy sight, O Lord, my strength, and my redeemer" (Ps. 19:14).

# 6

# No Such Thing
# as an Overnight Success

**K**ing David was old and lying in bed. He had served, fought and built, and now he was tired. He no longer had the heat or the fire within him to go out and win battles.

The Word tells us that he was cold and could not get warm. Poor circulation, I guess. Too bad they didn't have people around to sell him anti-everything vitamins to help him out.

In David's last days he could no longer fight battles as he once did. Instead, he dictated to his scribes the remarkable exploits he had accomplished during his life. In 2 Samuel 23:8-39 he recalls thirty-seven mighty men who had served with him and done incredible things.

During the course of his life, David had many relationships. Some of his associates were in deep despair, and some of them were deep in debt. One even acted as though he liked him but tried to throw a spear at him when he wasn't looking. But David nurtured relationships with many men who proved to be lifelong friends. These men would give their lives for him.

David was able to inspire men to greatness. He was not jealous of the call or the anointing on their lives but rather encouraged them to excel.

Of the thirty-seven great men that King David wanted remembered, he singled out three of them as heroes. The first one that David mentioned, he called the chief of the three heroes.

## Spell It? I Can't Even Pronounce It!

In David's eyes, Josheb-basshebeth Adino the Tachmonite, was the greatest of all his mighty men. He is not well-known among Bible readers, I'm sure. Many parents have named their children after such people in the Bible as Jonathan, Caleb, Samuel, Elisha and Noah. However, I don't know of anyone who named their little boy Josheb-basshebeth.

There is a good reason why we have not heard great sermons about this man. It's because he is an unknown man. When in ministry, one of the greatest temptations is the desire to be known.

When we first began our ministry, we attended numerous meetings of groups of men and women who had prophetic callings and anointings and were just getting organized. The inner circle of ministries was called "The Company of Prophets." It was considered an honor to be a part of that core group. But participation was by invitation only, and we were not invited.

I was devastated that we were not going to be a part of the "in" group. But a beacon of hope flickered when I heard they were forming the next level down, which would be called the "Sons of the Prophets." It wasn't really the dream team, but we would have to settle for that group. Would you believe it? We were not invited to join that group, either!

The Lord spoke to me so sweetly and said, "Daughter, be willing to be unknown. Be willing to do just what I tell you to do so that you can accomplish what I, the Lord your God, want to do in you."

What is the difference between a well-known and an unknown person? When you are known, everyone wants you to come and speak because you are sure to draw a crowd. When you are unknown, you usually wind up going to places uninvited, and that in itself is scary. You go because God commanded you to. You are a Tachmonite for God. There are many unknowns who have fought great battles and done great exploits for God.

I was sitting in my hotel room after a tremendous conference. The people who attended loved God and appreciated the ministry, and I was showered with many thanks and words of appreciation.

As I was resting in a nice, big, comfortable chair, I turned to my mother and said, "I have a nagging fear of getting all my rewards here on earth. I fear that when I get to heaven, everyone else will receive enormous crowns to throw at Jesus' feet and I will have only a rhinestone Jesus pin to throw. I can hear myself asking the Lord if there is anything else for me, and He lovingly says, 'Remember all those fruit baskets they brought to your motel room? Well that's it!' Mom set me straight with one look, and the Holy Spirit reminded me that I would "reap if I fainted not."

For an unknown person, invitations aren't plentiful even if you have the good fortune to fellowship with just the right people. Many Christians tell me that they feel they have great ministries and that they are just waiting to be discovered. It doesn't happen that way. Are you willing to

69

bow down and wash feet if necessary? Some believers want a place of honor, so they sit and wait until just the right invitation comes along.

The greatness of God is within all of us. We have so much potential, yet we wait for men to recognize it and come to us with a tremendous opportunity. The only way you will achieve anything for God is to go low, low, low!

One of the most dreaded comments anyone hears in a traveling ministry comes when someone hands you an envelope and says, "God bless you. I wish it could have been more." I have always wanted to smile and say, "I accept gifts by mail." But I realize then, and always, that God is my source.

For many years we were on the road for weeks, and our love offerings were just enough to get us to the next meeting. We can look back now and see the lesson that God was trying to teach us. We learned that the ministry is not a profession. It is a calling that causes us to bend low and allow Christ to flow from our hearts so that His people can be touched by His presence and Holy Spirit.

I am telling you this to encourage you and give you hope. You may think, *If only I were single, or if only I were younger, or older, or not tied down with little kids, or my job didn't stink, or my husband or wife were more understanding.* No! You are exactly what the Father is looking for — an unknown man or woman, ready to do whatever God asks through the power of the Spirit. When you've done that, God will elevate you.

What did this nobody, Josheb-basshebeth the Tachmonite, do? He slew eight hundred Philistines at one time (see 2 Sam. 23:8)! This was a supernatural, superhuman act. He decided he was going to do something for his God and his king. He didn't take on just one at a time — you know, easy does it. He attacked the whole army at one time and prevailed. He had to begin, press in and dig deep.

70

Beloved, don't read these words, lay them aside and wait for another time to begin your battle. You've put it off too long. There may not be another moment like this for you to touch Him and be broken in His presence. It won't be the same next week or next month. The time is now!

## I Would Be a Better Servant If It Weren't So Painful

I often struggle with the pressure of traveling every weekend while at the same time trying to be a good mother to my six children, a wife and lover to my husband, a friend, and a good daughter to my parents. Many times I am completely overwhelmed.

I was recently in an airport with our infant daughter, Lydia, in my arms. The airline representative asked me what my final destination was. My sleep-deprived brain just couldn't grasp the question or give a coherent reply. Instead, I began to cry. I couldn't remember my final destination. I couldn't even remember what city I was in. I really believe the man thought I had a severe case of postpartum depression. Yet, that very evening, standing on the platform before thirteen hundred people who were eagerly awaiting a revelation from God, the Holy Spirit within me rose up, and I gave a word with a fresh anointing.

The Word often uses the phrase "he rose up" in reference to David's second great hero, Eleazar. The name means "God helps me." Now this man did something amazing. He attacked the Philistines until his hand grew weary and was frozen to the sword (see 2 Sam. 23:9-10).

What did Eleazar do? He rose up, refusing to be intimidated by a group of soldiers. He got tired, but he never let go of his sword. By the time he was done fighting, his sword was part of him and his hand was frozen around it. He couldn't let go.

For years we have been taught about spiritual warfare —

71

how to fight the devil, conquer the enemy and do great things for God. We have learned that we have authority in Jesus, claimed our right to the covenant and memorized thousands of Scripture songs, but we have failed to grasp the sword like Eleazar did.

About ten years ago, when we were pastoring a small church in Central Florida, it was popular to have 6 A.M. prayer meetings. So we joined the crowd. I enjoyed seeing all those people who had looked so gorgeous on Sunday look so haggard at six on Monday morning!

It was obvious that they had dragged something out of the closet in the dark and dashed outside. Usually it was a food-stained T-shirt with a Scripture on it and mismatched shorts. None of them had time to put in their contact lenses because most of them had overslept. They sure looked comical in glasses that appeared to be leftovers from the fifth grade. And we won't even discuss hair!

My husband insisted that we stand as we prayed even though I pointed out to him that showing up at all was entirely voluntary. He knew very well that if we sat down, we would all soon be asleep. So there we were, twenty ugly but dedicated Christians, marching around in a circle, singing and putting on the armor of God.

Our hearts were right, but there came a time when many of the things we did were automatic and not of the Spirit. A similar situation exists in the lives of many believers today — their intentions are good, but their actions are automatic and not prompted by the Holy Spirit.

## Choose Your Weapon

Not long ago, I heard a woman share a vision she had experienced many years earlier. It was so powerful that she still remembered it in detail.

In the vision she saw herself standing in an armory. She

72

was fully equipped, having the shield of faith in her left hand, the breastplate of righteousness on her chest, the belt of truth strapped around her waist and her feet shod with the gospel of peace. The only thing missing was her sword.

The Lord spoke to her and said, "Daughter, I am going to give you the choice to select the right sword."

She went into the weapons chamber where she saw a large case in which there were twelve swords in a row. They were of every size and weight, and each bore a different design fashioned by a master craftsman.

She was immediately drawn to the sword in the middle. It was so beautiful, and it shone with a light from within. It was for her! She reached out to pick it up, but the moment she wrapped her hand around the handle she felt a sharp pain. The handle of the sword was cutting into her flesh.

She decided she could not fight with a sword that caused her such pain. She had to have one that was comfortable and fit her weight and height exactly. She needed one that helped her to be agile. She sought and found just such a sword. It fit her hand like a glove, and now she was ready to do battle.

When she went into the darkness with her sword, the demons and devils scowled at her from all sides though she was fighting with all of her might. She was doing all the right things, just as she was taught, just as she had studied. She knew how to stand, thrust, duck and fight. However, nothing happened. The devils remained in spite of all her screaming and yelling and fighting.

She fell to the ground, totally spent. She had exhausted herself fighting for God. This great woman of God hung her head in defeat. Devastated, depressed, she cried out to God and said, "Oh, God, something is wrong with me. I can't even fight for You. What should I do?"

The Lord spoke gently to her, showing her the sword she had refused. "Take that sword, the one you turned away from because of the sharp handle."

As she took it, it cut her flesh. She grasped it in both hands, and it cut deeper, but she tightened her grip because she knew that she had to outfight the enemy. In agony and pain she stood, able only to lift the sword in the air. She couldn't thrust, jab or even walk. To her great surprise, the devils fled.

Why must we carry a sword that causes pain? Because we have no power unless it cuts us. It separates the flesh from the spirit — not a process we enjoy. Eleazar's sword was in his hand, and it had to be pried from his hand when the battle was finished.

It does not matter how great we are or how wonderfully we write, teach, sing, pray or whatever else we do. We can recite all the right verses. We can remember all the Scripture songs we learned, all the things we have studied. We can rebuke with all our might, but if we do not allow the sword to separate the flesh from the spirit, we have no power. I cannot fight any devil in the flesh. Without the Spirit of God, I cannot overcome anything or anyone.

Circumcision of the heart is not a mental exercise. It's something that you feel, and it hurts.

Many of you are feeling defeated. It saddens me to see so many Christians who never find what they are looking for. Many ministries are never fulfilled because they choose the easy way, the sword that fits the hand perfectly but does not bring victory. We tend to drop the sword that cuts and hurts. But that is the one that wins the battles.

## Shammah — He Who Hears

Another one of David's heroes was Shammah. The word tells us that he was the son of Agee. With a name like that, Shammah must have learned to fight early in life. In the natural, he was not all that great. In the spiritual, he stood head and shoulders above Arnold Schwarzenegger or John Wayne.

A pastor friend called us a few years ago, nearly in tears. His church was in an upheaval and about to split. The reason for this terrible calamity — the color of the paint for the new sanctuary! One group demanded that it be blue, the other group green. Isn't it amazing what some Christians choose to fight about? Through the years we've heard similar stories — just substitute the word "paint" with "carpet" or "pew cushions" or a dozen other equally ridiculous things that have no bearing on eternity.

When do we fight? Shammah's name gives us the answer. His name means "he who hears." Hears what? Hears from God. Shammah's great exploit was defending a field of lentils in the midst of a Philistine attack when all the other Israelites fled (see 2 Sam. 23:11-12). Why would a grown man, a brave warrior, stand alone in a field of peas? He would certainly have to love lentils a lot to put his life on the line to defend them. What was it then? It was the principle of the battle: either to fight or to yield to an enemy, give up territory and come under subjection. We are told not to "give place to the devil" (Eph. 4:27) but to "fight the good fight of faith" (1 Tim. 6:12). Shammah was listening to God.

Sometimes in our relationships we find ourselves standing alone like Shammah. For whatever reason, we are deserted. Shammah could have thrown down his sword and said, "Forget it. I'm not going to risk my life if you don't care enough to help." The fact is that if God tells us to stand, we are not alone, and victory is certain.

The Philistines came to fight and destroy Israel, and the Israelites did what they usually did — they fled. Shammah, being a faithful soldier to David and Israel, stood up to the Philistines. Against all natural odds, he just said yes. I pray that that same spirit will come on all my kids!

Shammah stood in the midst of the lentil field and

defended it. The rest of the Israelites fled because they did not think it was very noble to die for a bushel of lentils. They might be willing to die for a big cause. But who wants to die for a bunch of peas or carrots or potatoes?

Often as Christians we are too willing to give up our vegetable gardens. We give up on our marriages, our kids, our friends and our churches. These are things close to home that God has given us, and instead of tending to them we ask for the nations. We sing a lot of songs in church about God giving us the nations. When was the last time you sang a song on Sunday about your family members: "fill my family with the Father's glory" or "flood my family with grace and mercy"?

Perhaps you said to yourself last week, "I am going to leave this church and never come back under any circumstances." You need to rethink your relationship with your families, natural and spiritual. To paraphrase an oft-quoted scripture, "What would it profit a person to gain the whole world and lose your own family?" (see Mark 8:36).

Every one of us has a God-given possession right here in our hands. What will you do with your possession? Does it seem worthy in your eyes — each time the enemy comes in — to be willing to die for your husband, your children, your wife? Is it a worthy cause to take a stand to protect your church? Is it worth it to you to protect your vegetable garden?

I teach, preach, minister and prophesy, but the greatest thing I do is fight for my vegetable garden. I have fought long and hard. So hard that God is enlarging my garden! God cannot give us the nations until we claim our families, because families are nations! Nations are not flags and borders on maps but multitudes of families — beginning with our family, one family at a time.

Many times I have stood in my vegetable garden, and people have said to me, "You can't do that; you can't do this." They have told me that what I was doing was crazy or that it was impossible and I shouldn't do it. Listen: If your dreams don't scare you, then they are not big enough!

"What do you mean you're adopting a black baby? You can't do that!" But I did. If I had listened to all the reasons why we couldn't or shouldn't adopt and raise children of color, I believe we would still have aching hearts and just one child. If I had listened to the naysayers, we wouldn't have five beautiful, chosen children now.

Once when the devil tried to destroy my family, many people advised me just to give up and walk away — call it a bad decision, and forget it. But I didn't, and I'm glad. All I knew how to do was rise up. But I stood firm. Not claiming, but defending what God had already given to me. Some people don't defend anything. They keep repossessing the same thing over and over again.

Maybe you don't know what to defend anymore. That's because your vegetable garden no longer has worth in your eyes. If it has no value, why would you want to defend it? What would be the benefit of dying for it?

## So What Are We Going to Do Now?

What then are the lessons here? Are we serving God only for the recognition, the pats on the back — or can we serve him like Adino the Tachmonite, with little or no recognition? In spite of all our accomplishments we must serve faithfully and quietly or ever become the squeaking wheel demanding to be greased in our relationships with others.

Like Eleazar we need to let the sword of the Word operate on our own flesh. Too often I see Christians destroy relationships by using the Word to club their fellow Christians into submission while not allowing the same Word to humble and correct their own lives. Hold fast to the sword as Eleazar did, even though it cuts into you, and you are weary, and the battle is difficult.

Is it worth it to stand alone in your field when everyone else is fleeing? When you are attacked from before and behind, do you still stand your ground?

Determine to stand like Shammah in the midst of your pea patch and defend it with all your might. Defend your spouse, your children and your church.

Don't ever think you have nothing to offer. Ask God to open your eyes. Ask Him to show you the value of your potatoes, carrots and parsley. They are your possessions. Take them and rise up in the power of the Holy Ghost.

# 7

# I Could Serve the Lord Better If It Weren't for the Other Christians

I was sitting at my computer working to meet a deadline that I had already missed. As usually happens just before I'm about to minister, someone in our household came along to provoke me.

It really takes a lot to get me to the point of losing control, but this time I went over the edge. I took that laptop lid and slammed it down. Then with the special anointing I have for saying cutting things and slashing someone to bits, I was about to let loose. What I had to say was truth, and I was going to set the person free with it. (I must add that Randi has been trying to deliver me from this "anointing.")

The Holy Spirit spoke to me and said, "Cathy, how you respond to this will determine whether I'm going to take you to the next level." My mouth was open, ready to speak angry words with tears in my eyes. I stopped mid-breath and said, "I'm sorry."

I didn't realize that walking in God's glory was directly related to how I walked with God in my relationship to others.

We've talked about our relationships with others in previous chapters. Now we will explore the importance of seeing God's glory in and through difficult relationships. Often, we don't see how they are related.

Recently, a friend told me about his uncle who is very, very rich. He owns one of the most exclusive restaurants in all of the United States, and as you might expect, one of the most expensive. My friend visited his wealthy uncle's restaurant and ordered what he thought would be a modest meal. You guessed it; when he got the check he nearly fell off his chair. It was exorbitant, to say the least. When I asked if his uncle gave him a break his reply was, "Not one red cent."

Sometimes Christians act as if their heavenly Father is like this very wealthy but very miserly uncle. A relative, yes, but not one who cares to help us. The Bible teaches us that just the opposite is true.

The word of the Lord for you in this chapter is comfort. "Comfort, comfort my people, says your God. Speak tenderly to Jerusalem" (Is. 40:1-2, NIV).

God wants to bring comfort to your heart. We think we understand how much God loves us and how much He is committed to helping us. But we feel it's up to us to help God do the work in us that He actually could do much better without our interference.

We need to experience the overwhelming power of God's love in our lives, especially when we have "blown it," in order to flow in that same love toward others who have made the same mistakes.

We need to understand that God is for us, not against us. He is committed to helping us. He longs to lift the burden and answer our prayers and deliver us. He says, "I take delight in the prosperity of my children." If you think your being poor delights God's heart, you're wrong. It doesn't delight your heart, does it?

Jesus was not a poor man. He was made poor that we might be made rich, but not poor in the way we think — walking around in tatters. His followers took care of Him, and I'm certain they gave to His treasury. When the Word says He didn't have anywhere to lay His head, it doesn't mean He didn't lay His head down. It just means that His name wasn't on the mortgage. God wants you to know that He is committed to taking you from where you are to a higher place. He is not dangling you over hellfire to see how much you can squirm, trying to get you to say, "All right, I give!" What does He require? He requires a simple act of faith.

One day when I was feeling low in spirit, my three-year-old came in with his little pink guitar, singing, "And the skies are not cloudy all day." Just a little song from him, maybe, but that's what the kingdom of God is, a place "where never is heard a discouraging word." He prophesied the word of the Lord to me.

What is God asking for? He's asking for something on the inside to rise up and say, *Lord, I believe. Help Thou my unbelief.* He's looking for a heart of faith that says, *You have not left me out here all by myself saying, I don't know what I'm going to do.* It doesn't matter how serious your situation is.

> Comfort, comfort my people...Speak tenderly to Jerusalem, and cry to her that her warfare is ended (Is. 40:1-2, RSV).

Do you claim that for your promise today? Your time of warfare is ended.

Some Christians are always worried. I believe in spiritual warfare, and I thank God for the ability to do battle. However, I get tired of being at war.

Not long ago my brother was assigned to a ship that was sent to Bosnia, but he stayed for less than a year. He had a certain time to serve, and then they brought him home. Some of us in the body of Christ think we're at war continually. There is a time when God says, "Your time of warfare has ended. You have a sabbatical. I'm pulling you off the front line for you to rest, sit in the shade, put your feet up, drink lemonade, count the stars and enjoy life for a little while."

I told a woman in the body of Christ that she needed to loosen up and learn to have fun. I told her she was more spiritual than Jesus is. "Your husband is miserable because you're no fun. You're always 'woo-wooing' in the Spirit, wondering what God is doing now and what He will do next. You need to know how to go out for a hamburger and laugh a little with your husband. You are absolutely no fun to be with."

I believe that there is a real devil out there. He is no fun, and he means business. He is ruthless. We need to be sober and vigilant, but the Word says that God Himself sits in the heavens and laughs. Many Christians are too serious.

I believe in having a good time. With all my kids, I have to. One day when we were watching *Beauty and the Beast* together, I danced with my sons to the music. I picked them up, and we waltzed around the house.

## Learning What to Expect From Our Relationship

A voice of one calling: "In the desert prepare the way for the Lord...Every valley shall be raised up" (Is. 40:3-4, NIV).

Anyone in the valley? Just cry out and say, "Lift me up, Lord." Every valley will be lifted up and every mountain and hill made low. Some of you have high highs and low lows. You don't know anything in between. Not every experience has to be a valley or a mountaintop. Sometimes it's just life. Not everything is either God or the devil. "The devil just blew out my tire, and it's flat. Oh, that devil." No! It was a nail that did it. It's just life; it's stuff; it just happens.

> And the crooked shall be made straight, and the rough places plain (Is. 40:4).

Do you have a lot of rough places? Make them a plain.

> And the glory of the Lord shall be revealed, and all flesh shall see it together: for the mouth of the Lord hath spoken it (Is. 40:5).

We are seeing the glory of the Lord today. There are some folks in Jacksonville who have meetings called "Fire and Glory." They just get together and sing, laugh and cry.

Can you remember the first time you were touched by God? You can't forget it. Do you long for that experience again? You don't want to go back in time, because you paid a big price to get where you are right now. But you want a renewal of that touch.

You have heard that God will never share His glory with another. That's scriptural. But you need to go back and research that scripture. We take it out of context and apply it to people we think are getting too big for their britches. God was referring to false and foreign gods. The apostle said that this was a mystery, "Christ in you, the hope of glory" (Col. 1:27). If He didn't want me to have this glory, why would Paul say that?

I'm a glory junkie. I'm a power junkie. I want the glory of God. I want the anointing of God. And however it manifests itself, I don't care, I want it. If I laugh, cry, pray, travail, sit quietly or run around the church, I just want the glory of

God. There is a glory that comes from on high to us individually, but there is a greater glory, a corporate glory, that comes when we are gathered in one place and God sovereignly comes and touches us and fills the room and stirs our spirits.

But there's another kind of glory. It's the glory that comes from within, the mystery glory. Christ in us, being released and revealed. I can go to a meeting, and if His anointing is there I can be stirred. But if I do not learn the greater glory, the mature glory of Christ *in* me, then I'm stirred but not changed. I want to be changed from glory to glory to glory. That's the glory that comes from within, not from without. It comes from going through trials, temptations, bitter circumstances and attacks from the enemy and by continually saying, "But God's Word has said..."

Isaiah was in the temple the year that King Uzziah died. The word says, "I saw also the Lord sitting upon a throne, high and lifted up, and his train [His glory] filled the temple" (Is. 6:1). Isaiah wasn't alone in the temple. Others were there with him. But they were all busy mourning over the death of King Uzziah. When the glory of the Lord was revealed only one man saw it — Isaiah.

You've got to look beyond the circumstances, death, pressure and your trials. When God is lifted up, His glory fills the place. We are the temple of the Holy Ghost, and His glory can fill that temple as well.

Isaiah 60:1 tells us to arise. There is something about simply arising. You don't need to learn fifteen steps to an overcoming life. You just need to arise. Get up and be sure you are standing up on the inside as well as on the outside.

Some things don't change even though you've walked with Jesus for many years. Some principles don't change, whether you are a veteran Christian or a new believer. Arise. Pull yourself up. Stand up. From what? From the depression that circumstances have put you in. Circumstances and resulting depression will keep you down.

To depress means to push upon something. You need to arise. The Bible doesn't say, "Bind the devil for four hours, or call sixteen intercessors and have them stand with you. Nor does it say, "Stay home from church and watch your favorite television pastor. Going is too hard, and today you don't want to be with happy people who are just a bunch of hypocrites anyway."

The Word tells us to *get up*. You're down there because circumstances have forced you down. But you don't have to stay there. Get up! Arise.

And shine. Be radiant, for your light has come and the glory of the Lord has risen upon you. The glory of the Lord will never come upon you if you don't get up. It will never be released in you if you will not arise. If you stay in your circumstances, you'll never see the glory of the Lord come. The glory of the Lord is on a higher plane.

"For behold, darkness shall cover the earth, and thick darkness the peoples; but the Lord will arise upon you, and his glory will be seen upon you" (Is. 60:2, RSV). There is a darkness covering the earth. It's not getting better; it's getting worse. What I see on television these days sickens me. Sitcoms that used to be funny are now filled with perversion. For a Christian, there isn't much worth watching anymore.

The Bible says the Lord will fill all the earth with His glory. How is He going to do that? The glory of God is going to be on you, and the people are going to see it. The only glory your family and others will see is what is on you. If you're walking around depressed all the time, why would they ever want to come into the kingdom — plus give up their Sundays? If Jesus gives you no joy, and you have no fun in life, and you can't enjoy anything, I feel sorry for you. So life is hard. It was hard last week, last year. Still, the joy of the Lord is our strength.

What's God been doing in you in the last five years? It's called character development. He could have taken us right into the glory. Do you know why He didn't? Because there are generations to come.

I look back ten years and think how stupid I was then. I guess ten years from now, and until Jesus comes, I'll look back and remember how stupid I was. He has been working in my character. And He's been watching to see how you respond in certain situations. What are you doing in your marriage, with your money, at your job? Are you going to prevail and overcome? The devil tries to convince us that God wants to see how long we can dangle.

My husband often reminds me that the generous man will be made fat. In Hebrew, that means he will get the anointing; the generous man gets the anointing.

Why do we want the anointing? In it is everything we need. You don't have to have a pulpit ministry. Most of you will never have one, but you can affect people for the kingdom of God that I'll never be able to touch. You can go with the glory of God. All you have to do is walk into a room, and people will notice something about you that they just can't explain.

How do you get that glory? Pray, fast, give and do all those other things you know to do. But the Lord has been impressing me with this — they'll know that we're Christians because we have *love*.

If in the midst of a crisis a medical team administered a new drug to your husband to save his life and then told you he had a *reaction* to the medicine, you would know that was bad news.

But if they told you that your husband *responded* to the treatment, you'd know that's good. Reaction is bad. Response is good. The Lord has been putting me in a responsive mood and taking me out of a reactive mood.

The mirrors in our bathroom extend from the sink to the

ceiling. When my husband brushes his teeth, he leaves toothpaste and water spots all over the mirrors. I think he takes his brush and flings the water off it and onto the mirror. It's gross, and I hate it. You men or women who live alone, rejoice!

One day — after I brought this to Randi's attention — I walked into the bathroom and was taken aback by my water-spotted mirror. I thought, *I cook when I'm home. I also go out and minister. I take time with my children in between meetings. Why do I have to put up with this mess?*

The Lord spoke to me and said, "You want the glory. Get the Windex." You see, we think the glory comes by going to the Philippines and having water drip on our heads from a leaking roof or having a dirty outhouse to use. However, we don't all get that opportunity. So, I got the Windex.

When my husband came home that afternoon, he said, "Honey, did you see how nice and clean I kept the mirrors?" I almost bit my tongue in half to keep from saying anything. Why? Because I want the glory of God in my life. I want God's presence with me always.

What have you been going through? I'm certain that more times than not, your suffering can be blamed on your tongue. Or your disobedience. Have you put up your fist toward God and said, "God, if You don't do something, I'll just die. If You really love me, why are You allowing this to happen to me? I wouldn't do this to someone I loved."

When I get provoked, I take it as a green light, not a red light. I've heard Christians say, "I guess this is God's way of closing the door." When I go through hard places I know I must be right on track, because the devil is really mad.

I often say, "God stops; the devil only hinders." If I recognize that I am only being hindered, I push ahead.

I know you will find this hard to believe, but Randi and I were having a disagreement. I thought I had made a good decision about something all on my own. In fact, I convinced

myself (and told him) I had made the decision for *his* benefit. I felt I was justified because I was being prudent and
helping *him*. I don't advise you to try this with your husband. It's not a good idea.

Randi was on a business trip when I made the monu-
mental decision, and when he returned home he was not
very happy. I reminded him of how much money I had
saved us, but he was not pacified. I know this never happens in your house, but we had a little yelling session — after
which I proceeded to prepare to minister at a huge, much-
advertised women's conference.

I told Randi that I was leaving for a meeting and would
probably never return home. (Of course he didn't buy that!)
A perfect frame of mind to begin a conference, don't you
think? I'm sharing this with you to let you know that you
too can have a relationship with God and be used by Him
even when you blow it.

I decided I couldn't leave the house in that condition.
What if I got hit by a train or some other horrible thing happened to me? So I walked across the room to where my
husband was sitting, knelt at his feet, put my head in his lap
and told him I was wrong in what I did. I asked him to forgive me. I was crying, because I knew I had hurt him.

When we hurt someone, we're sometimes glad because
we've struck back — especially if he has hurt us. You must
be able to say, "I'm sorry, I know I have hurt you." If the
person forgives you, praise God. However, he may reply,
"Some things will never change. Get off my back."

Randi put his arms around me and began to weep. He
said, "I just want us to be together in our decisions." And he
was right. I often go ôut on a limb because I think I'm
alone.

When I arrived at that women's conference, I felt the
greatest anointing I have experienced in all my years of
ministry. It didn't come by preaching the Word. That is what

you can *see*. The glory comes when you can't see me. The anointing comes when you can't see Cathy Lechner as a wife and mother, cooking tuna noodle casserole for the fourth day in a row.

The Lord spoke to me and said, "As long as you will stand together in unity and keep your heart right, there isn't anything that I won't do for you. Even if you and Randi both blow it, if you will humble yourselves and stand together, I'll do it."

You see, our relationship with each other reflects our relationship with our heavenly Father. The bridge of forgiveness over which we cross to forgive our family and friends is the same bridge over which forgiveness comes to us from the Father.

If you feel all alone but humble yourself, there isn't anything God won't do for you. He resists the proud, but He gives grace to the humble.

Do you want the glory of God? It comes when you are on the front line. It comes in relationships with one another.

Can you pray right now and ask God for His glory as you walk in forgiveness to any and all who have hurt you? God has forgiven them, and so can you.

Say yes, and see the glory of God in your life.

# 8

# Why Does It Still Bother You If You've Died to Self?

I will never forget one day when I needed a word from the Lord, and I knew exactly what I wanted Him to say to me: "Oh, Daughter, everything is going to work out wonderfully. You are going to drive a new Lincoln Town car. Your ministry will far surpass and then eclipse those around you. All of your enemies will meet with sudden destruction. You will get cuter and taller, and many people will begin to remark that you resemble Princess Diana."

That is not the word I received when Randi and I stood before Bishop Bill Hamon in Lake Worth, Florida, sixteen years ago. The word of the Lord to Randi was tremendous. The man of God began to speak with power, sharing the glorious things God would do for and through him.

Then it was my turn. If my husband received such a

wonderful report from the Lord, could mine be any less glorious? He began, "Daughter, submit, submit, submit." I could have crawled under the pew. I don't know what else he said, because I tuned him out after that. Once I got over the initial shock and surprise, I decided that Dr. Bill needed to be roasted on a slow rotisserie.

Looking back to that night, I can see that it was the night God marked me for service. Although we had already been in ministry for three years, that day something changed.

My experience was similar to that of an eighteen-year-old who thinks he knows everything and then signs up for military service. He finds himself right in the middle of basic training. In a span of eight weeks, the army takes him from being a boy to being a man. But it's eight weeks of misery, made up of little sleep and bad food. The military systematically strips that boy of his image and gradually replaces it with the military's image.

He is taught to trust and obey those in command over him. Nothing less than total obedience is acceptable, because one day lives will be dependent on his ability to obey orders.

Why is it that when we think about the promotion of the Lord, we equate it to easy times and great blessings? When you sign up for God's army, you're going to wake up in basic training someday. So don't let your position disappoint you.

## Who Would Want a Cool Drink From a Filthy Vessel?

Have you ever had a plumber come when your sink or toilet overflowed? One of my children once dropped scissors down the toilet, causing it to back up and overflow. I don't know why children do things like this. You see a little hand raised, ready to drop a large object into the toilet just so the child can watch it go down. Before you can yell

"Don't!" he's already dropped the object and flushed the toilet with a What-did-I-do-wrong? expression on his face.

We're like the backed-up toilet. Foreign objects get stuck in us, and all of a sudden the Spirit of God is not flowing. We realize we are not usable vessels for the Lord.

A pastor called me to talk about my meetings, even though I was not scheduled to speak in his church. The Spirit of God spoke to me and told me, "He is not calling for a meeting. He really wants a word from the Lord, but he doesn't want to come out and ask you for it." I sat there thinking to myself, *I really don't feel like ministering to him.* I was trying to feed the baby on my lap, I had a toothache, and I just didn't feel that I was sensitive enough to the Holy Spirit to minister right then. I made arrangements to talk with him later.

I fully realize that God wants us to be free-flowing vessels whether we feel like it or not. We can be going through the worst situations in our lives, yet we can still have the ear of the Spirit so we can minister to other people.

We are going to take a look at those things that block the blessings of God. We are going to look at those things that need to be unclogged so that we can fulfill our destinies. I want to know how to keep the Spirit flowing, even though it may be painful and even though it may be difficult.

I want to share with you the complications of the self-life. I don't usually go into this area, and if it doesn't fit, don't wear it. However, since we're talking about relationships, I need to mention this.

You are daughters and sons of destiny. There are daughters and sons of God who will not fulfill their destinies because they allow all manner of things to come into their lives to sidetrack them from the true vision that God has for them.

## Living On Emotions

One area where many of us falter is in our natural emotions. We allow other people and their negative attitudes to rule us.

Have you ever been annoyed or disgusted with someone and suddenly let him have it, forgetting momentarily that your image is to be recreated in God's image? I know I am guilty of doing just that. That is when I become aware of the amount of "self-love" that still lives.

The following are a few of the manifestations of the self-love.

## *Holding Grudges*

We are not going to make it without one another. There is too much work for just one person to do.

I was riding in a car with someone who brought up the name of a minister who had once spoken against us. They went on and on about how wonderful his ministry was and how terrific he was. As I sat there, I felt this thing in my throat wanting to come out in the form of words like, "Well, he's all right, but..." I couldn't believe what I really wanted to say. I thought I had gotten rid of all those negative feelings; it was hard to believe they were still there. I could hear the Lord say, "Swallow it." I sat in that back seat and swallowed hard. The Lord said, "If you sow it, Cathy, you will reap it in your own ministry."

So I said, "They are really terrific people. They have written some awesome books that really touched my life." Then I tried to think of some other nice thing to say, which wasn't easy.

My mother always told me, "If you can't say something good about someone, don't say anything at all." My silence for the rest of the ride was deafening. Do you know what we sometimes say in situations like that one? "You know, I can't say anything, but you just pray about it." What does that do in the heart of the listener? It plants a seed of suspicion.

## Being Overly Serious

We often take ourselves too seriously. We need to relax and enjoy our salvation.

When I was in the Philippines I had my first experience with a chamber pot. It was made for little Filipino bottoms, and the first time I used it, I was surprised by the suction. A friend had to sort of lower me on to it. Then, to my dismay, it sealed like a vacuum, and we couldn't remove it at first. After much tugging and pulling, I finally parted company with said pot.

I know that isn't the sort of thing missionaries write home about, but whenever I take a situation too seriously and start to lose my joy, the Lord reminds me of that chamber pot.

I love the movie *Matthew* which portrays Jesus as one who laughed. A commercial for the movie shows the lame man after he was healed, leaping into Jesus' arms. Together they fall to the ground and laugh and rejoice. I believe that's how Jesus really would have reacted. He knew how to laugh and rejoice.

## Pride

Pride results from an exalted view of our success, position, training, appearance or natural gifts and abilities. It manifests itself as a self-important, independent spirit.

Christian leaders have told me about the problems they have had with associates and staff members who were tremendously gifted but lost their anointing because of pride in their gift. They became problems instead of blessings.

## Love of Human Praise

There's a part of us that needs love and approval. But a sure sign of immaturity is the love of human praise and an unhealthy desire to be noticed. In a husband and wife relationship, we certainly need that love and approval. I am referring instead to an obsessive secret desire to be noticed. People infected with this desire love portraying themselves as an authority on the subject at hand. They try to draw attention to themselves in each and every conversation.

That's the kind of person who would boast, "I prayed for fifteen people, and three and a half of them fell down when I touched them and prayed for them. I know it wasn't me, but it *was* my hand!"

We long to be part of the "in" group. But if we are fulfilling our call in God, what does it matter? I don't even know which one is the "in" group anymore.

False humility is just as bad. It used to be that when people would compliment me on my singing, I would say, "Oh, it wasn't me — it was God. Give the glory to Him." And I would keep muttering about it not being me until one day the Lord said to me, "Be quiet and say thank you. They know it wasn't you. They are fully aware that it was God."

As we seek human praise, we continually draw attention to ourselves and our accomplishments. Even when we've had an outstanding time in the presence of the Lord, we swell with pride at the thought that God is revealing Himself to us more than to others. We may not say so in words, but our attitude shows it. We must be sensitive to the Spirit of the Lord and rejoice with those that are rejoicing and weep with those who weep. We may be in a "lofty" place, but we need to be sensitive to other people and what they are facing.

## Anger and Impatience

We must guard ourselves against the stirrings of anger and impatience, which we often wrongly label "nerves." Angry behavior results from a touchy, sensitive spirit and manifests as resentment or retaliation when we're contradicted or corrected. We're tempted to throw sharp, heated words at one another. Sadly, leaders can be the most guilty of this; they tend to be outraged and pick at flaws when they feel they've been overlooked or gone unnoticed.

What we so desperately need is a fresh touch of the Spirit of God, allowing Him to bathe us in His love. We need a humble, teachable, "I-don't-want-any-of-the-glory" spirit. A person who is willing simply to minister and then disappear — that's the kind of vessel God can use to accomplish mighty things.

A woman approached me after a meeting and asked me to forgive her. When I asked her why, she told me she had heard some unkind remarks concerning me and had based her entire opinion of my ministry on what she had heard. I was stunned at first and wanted to say something unkind in retaliation. But after giving it some thought, I told her, "I've done the same thing. I've heard and believed stories about ministries and people I have never met, and a seed was sown. Sister, no offense is taken." She had a sweet spirit, and God ministered to her and healed her that night as she wept.

I don't do it right all the time. But if I had chosen to take offense in that situation, I would have cut myself off from ministering to this child of God. The ditches are littered with people who had great anointings but became important in their own eyes. Samson himself was not even aware when the anointing left him (see Judg. 16:20).

## An Argumentative, Talkative Spirit

The Word says that when too many words are spoken, sin is inevitable. When you talk too much, there is a tendency to sin.

Talking all the time — I find myself doing that at times. After a while, my spirit starts grieving, and I need to retreat and be quiet.

Occasionally we meet someone who can slice us through with a harsh, sarcastic expression. Do you have a driving, commanding spirit? Are the words and phrases you speak laced with sarcasm and caustic wit? Do they wound and cut rather than help and heal?

By spewing out harsh, sarcastic expressions, some people attempt to intimidate and control others. This results in an emotional roller-coaster ride in their walk with God. And this spirit is found in both men and women.

A Jezebel spirit is not characterized by strength. It is signified by manipulation and control (see 1 Kin. 21:7-15). There are Christian women who have a driving and manipulating spirit, and their families would rather give in to them than go against them. They figure it's just not worth the fight.

God forbid that our husbands, wives or friends could label us Jezebels. We need to be compassionate and merciful toward those around us.

## A Peevish, Fretful Spirit

There are some who are continually fretful. They have a disposition that loves to be coaxed and humored, especially when the prophetic word is being ministered. *I'm just going to sit in the back. If she has a word for me she'll come get me. I'm going to wait until last, and when she's tired and drained and the ministry's over, I'll go up and tell her I can't take it anymore. I need a word.*

Christians with a fretful spirit need much counseling. I

don't do counseling. I'm a terrible counselor. I get provoked by people who week after week won't do what I tell them to. They sit in my office and tell me over and over about their problem. I ask, "Did you do what I asked you to do?"

They cry and say, "No, I just can't do that." Or they answer, "I've done all that already."

One time, after months of counseling, I told a suicidal woman, "Well, honey, then just go ahead and kill yourself, because you're the only person alive that Jesus and the Word do not work for." That was the last counseling appointment the church gave me.

We need to be aggressive with the enemy, but we also need to be ruthless with ourselves. A wise man's little folly is like a fly in the ointment. "A small mistake can outweigh much wisdom and honor. A wise man's heart leads him to do right, and a fool's heart leads him to do evil" (Eccl. 10:1-2, TLB). No matter how much good we have done, a little sin can cause our life to stink. We need to have a heart of repentance. It's much easier to follow than it is to lead, but God is looking for leaders, those who will mark the way.

I don't believe in unhealthy introspection — if we look hard enough, we can always find something wrong with ourselves. But when the Spirit of the Lord tells us to examine our hearts, we need to obey, repent and then let the Holy Spirit of God come and shine His beacon in our lives. You see, I care more about what He thinks of me than what you think of me. It's His opinion alone that matters.

## Carnal Fear

A man-fearing spirit causes us to be afraid of what other people might think about us. We shrink from reproach and duty because we are afraid. "What if I miss it? What if it isn't God?" Well, what if it is God? "What if it's not right?" But what if it is right?

98

I was invited to a pastors' meeting, but I didn't know any of the men present. However, I had been told before the meeting that many of those who would be attending were very well known in their circle of ministry. That *really* boosted my confidence.

The Lord gave me a word for one of the men there. He told me to tell this man of God that more and more doors where going to open for him to travel with Norvel Hayes. I thought, *Oh, God, what if I'm wrong? Because if I'm wrong, I'll be really wrong.*

The Lord said to me, "Cathy, speak what I put in your mouth. Let them judge the word."

So I told this man, "Brother, the Lord tells me that more and more, Norvel Hayes is going to ask you to go with him. You will do more ministry." Everyone in the room began to rejoice and praise God. They all knew this man and what his ministry was. He said to me, "Did you know that I travel and teach in Norvel Hayes' Bible school?"

What if I had been disobedient and not brought the word? The reason we don't bring the word is we're afraid of what people will think of us if we are wrong. I must say what I believe God has given me. You judge it, and if it's wrong, I'm willing to take correction. But if I'm right, then it's going to bless your socks off, and you'll never be the same.

Many of you are going to have the opportunity to minister, and it will cost you something to do it. It's going to draw on resources that you don't have. God is asking you to go, and you'll have to say, "Yes, Lord. Here am I; send me." Don't go to your checkbook to find out if you can afford to go. That just indicates that you are serving mammon. If your answer is yes, He will provide the means.

When a little church invited me to come the pastor apologized and said, "I don't know what we can do for you financially. We have only about thirty people, but we'll put our faith out and believe." Now when you go to a small church it's not really them putting their faith out; it's you putting your faith out so your needs will be met.

However, I prayed about going, and the Lord told me to go. He let me know I wasn't to base my decision on how many people were in the church or how much they could give. I was to go because He told me to. The reverse of that is that I don't automatically accept invitations from very large churches. Often they take up a love offering for you, and when you get home, you find out they didn't love you all that much.

You can't shrink from doing your whole duty. And you can't reason around it by favoring those of wealth or position. I admit that this is a touchy area. It's hard not to be nicer to those who can write you a check for five or ten thousand dollars at a whack. But that's a snare. You must listen to the Spirit of God and move according to where He calls you to go.

Some have a fear of doing or saying something that will drive a prominent person away. We're afraid of offending them. We need to be delivered from the faces of men and speak what God puts on our hearts to say.

## Jealousy

Jealousy, the Word says, is a spirit as cruel as the grave. Sometimes when we're being critical, we don't realize that we are actually jealous. We see how God is using someone else, and we would like to be used in the same manner. Seeing someone else prosper or otherwise blessed can cause resentment to rise within us. That's what makes it so difficult for singles when they see their friends getting married. They are happy for them, but they say in their hearts, *What about me, God?*

For years it seemed as if every woman I knew was getting pregnant except me. I would ask God, "Do you love them more than you love me? It's not fair. Don't I please you?" I was envious. I didn't want their babies, but why wasn't God blessing me? Wasn't I as faithful? I saw someone else getting the blessing that I wanted, and a spirit of jealousy rose within me. It's not wrong to want to see the promise of God come to pass, but when our desire causes us to become critical of other people, it's very wrong.

We hear singles say things like, "She shouldn't have married that man. I think she's foolish if you ask me. She hardly knows him," when they would give their right arm to be walking down the aisle with a man. You must be free from that kind of jealous thinking. A healthy reaction would be: "If she found somebody, there's got to be someone out there for me." Personally, I don't struggle with this. I have one husband, and that's enough — though I have asked him if he ever noticed that the Word says, "He who finds a wife finds a good thing" (Prov. 18:22, NAS).

We become envious of others when their gifts and talents are more appreciated than ours are. We get into a disposition that focuses on their faults or failings rather than on the gifts or virtues that others seem to be so focused on.

We say things like, "Oh yes, she is wonderful, but did you know she was married once before?" Or, "You know, he was thrown out of his last church." We just have to get that little dig in there instead of saying, "They are so awesome. God bless them and their ministry!" If they are in error, He doesn't need you to help Him correct it. I have enough trouble keeping Cathy Lechner on track without trying to keep everyone else in place.

Some of us sit under the leadership of people that we feel are less equipped than we are. We can do it better; our anointing is greater. But we need to be free from the desire to be front and center. Most of the people I know that are front and center didn't choose to be there. They just wanted to be a servant, and God thrust them out there. They fall apart when they have to make a simple announcement; they don't want to be the center of attention.

If you grab for ministry leadership, it won't come. I know Spirit-filled Christians who are driven by the desire to be up front. They desire to have their gift and ministry known — when what they really need to be doing is simply serving God.

## A Dishonest, Deceitful Disposition

Deceitfulness involves evading and covering the truth. "How many did you have in church on Sunday?"

"Well, somewhere between five and five thousand. Hallelujah! We don't know. The crowd just overwhelmed us."

We like our spirit to be rejuvenated, but our character has got to be developed. The Holy Spirit is a gentleman, and He will deal with your sin in secret if you will deal with it. But if you won't, He cares enough about you that He will reveal it to an intercessor and deal with it in public. Then if you still won't repent, He will reveal it to more intercessors until you're ready to confront it. Dear God, help us — and help the intercessors!

Last month a pastor friend of ours was sitting in the front row in a meeting when the Lord gave me a word for him, but I didn't know how to bring it forth. I told him I had a word for him and said, "Oh, Jesus, help me." His eyes got big, and he said, "Oh, Jesus, help me!"

God doesn't want to place you in a large group and tell you, "I saw last week when you lusted after that man in those tight blue jeans who took off his shirt and drank Pepsi down at that construction site." God doesn't want to embarrass you in public. He wants you to deal with those things in secret. He wants to tell you how much He loves you. I have learned that when God reveals the secret sin of another to me while I'm praying, my first response has to be, "Lord, is there any of that in me?"

I've seen intercessors destroy churches because they started glimpsing things in the Spirit and tried to put together the big picture from the little bit God revealed to them. They spread their theories throughout the church and split it wide open. The Word says when you strike the shepherd, the sheep scatter.

Intercessors, you have a grave responsibility. Some intercessors that I have known were nutty, just plain weird. I wanted to keep my distance from them because they would get some weird, wacko word and ruin twenty people's lives with it. On the other hand, there are true, absolutely pure intercessors. There is a fine line between criticism and the discerning of spirits. We can enter into the spirit realm and learn things about people, but we had better see our own faults in the person who has been misbehaving. We then humble ourselves and keep our mouths shut until God gives the go-ahead to speak to that person in meekness and humility. I have heard of people who marched into the pastor's office with a pointed finger and made accusations that brought destruction.

## Hurt and Resentment

Some of you are in really difficult relationships that you have to deal with every day. Someone once asked me, "How often do you have the opportunity to get offended?"

I asked him, "Are you married?" Even two Christians who love God and each other will offend one another without realizing it. We have to deal with offense. We have to tell the devil, "You have nothing in me. If He is in me, He can use me to destroy you" (see John 14:30).

I know many people who minister with an angry spirit. They prophesy out of anger. One lady prophesied over me, and it was horrible. I had closed a women's conference on Saturday night. Sunday morning I was seated on the platform with two ministers of the church, and as I was getting ready to go to the podium to speak to the large congregation, a woman came down the aisle with her Bible turned to Jeremiah and began to prophesy. "And there are false prophets in the land," she said, Then she turned around, pointed her bony finger at me and added, "And they will *die!*"

Since she was pointing directly at me, I figured she meant me. She was full of the spirit of anger and used the Bible as a weapon.

You can always find scriptures that will support your anger. There are a lot of angry people who speak against the church with venomous words. Jesus loves His church and gave Himself for His church. He chastens those He loves, but He doesn't beat them to death. We can't minister out of an angry spirit because we are mad at people. Even a word of rebuke must come from a heart of love.

How do you discipline your children? Because you love them you don't beat them and throw them out the door. If you discipline them correctly, after you have spanked them, you hug them and dry their tears. You tell them that the reason you must correct them is because you love them. Jesus loves us that same way.

When you get a pedicure, a file is used to scrape the callouses. Let the Spirit of God scrape the callouses from your life until you can say, "I'm willing. Do what You want in my life. Say what You have to say to correct me so I can be used by Your Spirit." Don't remain toughened so that the Spirit of God can't enter in and do His work.

Deal with the truth when you are confronted with it. Have a spirit that says, "I want to be teachable," even when you are confronted with criticism that you don't like, criticism that wounds you. The word says, "Faithful are the wounds of a friend" (Prov. 27:6).

## Unbelief

In times of pressure or opposition, unbelief can lead to discouragement. The Word calls unbelief the "slander of God." You must never cop out when the going gets tough. You can do it, but if you do, you won't see your promise come to pass.

Unbelief is a lack of quietness and confidence in the Lord. A believer who maintains a quiet confidence in the Lord is not out there screaming at demons, not out there binding everything. Their confidence in the Lord will not allow them to be dissuaded from God's love toward them. They know that in spite of any situation, God loves them. They will press on whether they see the promise come to pass today, tomorrow, next week or next year.

Lack of faith and trust in God — the children of Israel had that. They didn't have that submissive, yielded spirit that says, "I want to do what You want me to do, even though it's not easy."

There is a disposition that causes a person to worry or complain in the midst of pain, poverty or even divine providence. A person with this disposition feels anxious about whether everything will come out all right. That's understandable if he is a baby Christian. But after you've walked with the Lord a few years, you should have that quiet confidence in your heart.

I remember sitting in my motel room after returning late from a meeting. I knew I would have only one day with my family before I had to leave again. I cried out, "Lord, it's so hard to leave my children. I can scarcely bear it." I was laying out before the Lord what I was feeling in my heart.

The Lord kept speaking to me, "If you'll just take up your cross and follow after Me, you'll see the glory of God." Time and time again, God has fulfilled that promise to me. He has blessed me beyond measure.

I will admit that 1994 was the darkest year of my life. But

it was the year that I saw the glory of God to the greatest extent. Oh, that I might know Him in the power of His resurrection as well as in the fellowship of His suffering! The hardest places always seem to be the sweetest. I don't know why that is, but I know it's true.

Today, with all the encouraging teaching tapes and books made available to us, it is a sin to worry. No doubt, you have heard and forgotten more than most of the world has yet to hear. We have to base our lives on the very premise that *He is with us!*

## Lack of Power With God

A lack of power indicates a lack of prayer life. If you do not pray, you will not have power. I'm not talking just about maintenance prayer, I'm talking about prayer that produces power to change people's lives. Effectual, fervent prayer produces power.

## Selfishness

The selfish love of money makes us lust for the easy life. Many people just want the financial battle to be over. They don't want to fight anymore; it's too hard. *If I could win the Reader's Digest Sweepstakes...*

Money is not the answer to our problems. If it were, the rich would be happy and have no worries.

Galatians 2:19-21 says: "For through the law I died to the law so that I might live for God. I have been crucified with Christ and I no longer live, but Christ lives in me. The life I live in the body, I live by faith in the Son of God, who loved me and gave himself for me. I do not set aside the grace of God, for if righteousness could be gained through the law, Christ died for nothing!" (NIV).

The law Paul is talking about here is the Ten Commandments. Basically, the law can be illustrated this way: A man wakes up in the morning, rubs his face and feels stubble. He thinks, *I really need to shave. But maybe I can get by without doing it.* Then he sees himself in the mirror and says, "I really need to shave. It's worse than I thought." But he doesn't break the mirror and begin to shave with it.

The mirror is the law. We assess ourselves and think, *I'm not so bad. I'm certainly not as bad as some other people I know. Actually, I think I'm pretty good. I try to do what's right. I pay my tithes.*

Then we go to the Word and see what it says, and we say, "I'm worse than I thought I was." We don't take the Word and slice ourselves to bits with it. The letter of the law kills. The Word is the mirror that shows us what our true condition is. It shows us our need for cleansing.

There are areas of our lives that need adjusting. When you look at these areas in your own life, your prayer should be, "Lord, I can't adjust on my own. I see my true condition as revealed by Your Word. Holy Spirit, help me to adjust any area that needs it."

# 9

# Charm School of the Holy Spirit

Do you remember the rules of etiquette your mother taught you as a child? "Always say please and thank you." "Be sure you have on clean underwear in case you are in an accident." "Eat everything on your plate, including your brussel sprouts, because there are children in China who are starving." And the classic, "Never blow your nose into your hand and wipe it on your sleeve."

We were given rules for every area of our lives. Rules for eating such as, "Close your mouth when you're chewing; I don't want to see it twice." "Don't talk with your mouth full; you just hit me with a lima bean."

We had special rules when company came. "Never, ever, discuss our Sunday morning car conversation in front of Pastor and Mrs. Brimsnod again!"

Then there was bathroom etiquette...oh well, let's skip that one. I'll assume you passed the course.

As we grew older, our lessons changed. There were dating rules, wedding rules, in-law rules, even drinking-out-of-the-milk-carton rules. (Don't do it or your mother will smack you.) For every phase of life there seemed to be a pre-scribed behavior, concluding with going to your Great-uncle Pinrod's funeral: "Don't make a pig of yourself at the buffet table; don't talk too loud; don't try to raise him from the dead, and positively, under no circumstance are you to touch Uncle Pinrod!"

Church attendance held its own set of rules. It did not matter what faith you were or what you believed — we all had acceptable worship guidelines.

## Can I Get Up Now?

In the mid-eighties, I was introduced to falling down under the power of the Holy Spirit. The people in my particular denomination did not fall down in church. We knelt down and sat down, but we definitely did not fall down. We did have a dear brother in the congregation, Brother Shundi, that would get blessed, mostly during the Sunday evening evangelistic service. He would take off running around the church to the strains of "I'll Fly Away," shouting "Hallelujah" with sweat dripping down his face.

Our pastor, who also happened to be my father, would say something like, "Well, praise God, Brother Shundi is really getting blessed tonight." We had running, but alas, no falling.

The first time I ever experienced "falling under the power of the Holy Spirit" was during an incredible time when God was moving in my life. An evangelist laid her hand on me, and I simply could not continue to stand, the power of the Holy Spirit was so strong.

As I was falling forward instead of backward, I remember thinking, *At least no one has to catch me.* It's really embarrassing when you are being prayed for and the two original catchers call for a backup.

Lying face down on the floor, I began to worship the Lord. After a few minutes in that position the sweat on my face began to mingle with the carpet fiber. Turning my head from side to side became painful. Then I noticed rug burn developing on my cheeks and forehead. That happens when you don't get caught.

*How long should I lie here?* I wondered. *If I jump up too fast, I might not look very spiritual, and it may hurt the evangelist's feelings. However, if I lie here too long, people will begin to notice how large certain areas of my body are and — oh no! — the rug burn is beginning to spread.*

It's odd that no one ever taught us the "falling down under the power rules." Surely there's a protocol manual called *Falling Down 101* somewhere.

Seriously, though, I've found that there is a training manual for the Charm School of the Holy Spirit. It begins in 2 Peter.

> Grace and peace be yours in abundance through the knowledge of God and of Jesus our Lord. His Divine power has given us everything we need for life and godliness through our knowledge of him who called us by his own glory and goodness. Through these he has given us his very great and precious promises, so that through them you may participate in the divine nature and escape the corruption in the world caused by evil desires (1:2-4, NIV).

In this short passage, Peter begins our charm training by telling us that two of the most important traits in any believer are grace and peace — grace being God's unmerited favor and peace being calm, quiet rest, stillness and tranquility.

Peter is exhorting us to begin to use our faith for things that are eternal. Material things are good, but they are temporary. Character changes are better, and they bring eternal results.

## Where Is the Magic in Your Magic Lamp?

My mother purchased a lamp at a local discount store and invited the family to her house for its inauguration. Gathering us into her bedroom, she whispered, "My new lamp...it's magic." Then she touched the base, and the lamp shone brightly. A chorus of oooh's and aahh's that were usually reserved for really great Christmas presents or new grandchildren came bursting forth from all of us as she touched the lamp base again and again. Each time the light shone brighter, and we were very impressed.

A year later, this same mother took a box of stuff to church to sell at a fund-raiser. Carelessly thrown on top of the box was her precious "magic lamp." I couldn't believe it. Only one year before she had practically offered baskets of fruit and burnt offerings to it. Now it lay in a heap. Seeing my look of horror and disbelief, she casually said, "Lightning hit it. The only way it will light up is to plug it in manually. All the magic is gone." And that was that!

Things are nice to have. God wants us to have nice things, but they do not bring peace. Grace and peace come from an intimate relationship with Jesus.

Peter said that God has already given us everything we need (see 2 Pet. 1:3). It's been granted, bestowed, placed inside of you. You have everything you need to live with your husband, your wife, your children, your job — to face any situation that does not seem to respond to your pleading, prodding or even your prayers.

Frequently I hear people in the prayer line say, "I just can't take it anymore."

My answer to them is not without compassion, but I ask them, "If you can't take it anymore, what is your alternative? Are you going to walk away from Jesus, run off with Bubba and sin for awhile? You'll be back in five years with a broken heart. Of course you can take it." You already have in you all that you need for every situation.

His promises are true, and they cost Him much — His life. Peter encourages us that by "his great and precious promises" we have already won (2 Pet. 1:4, NIV). In other words, God's great and precious promises will actually take you through life's difficulties and temptations and bring you out with victory on the other side. His promises will cause you to soar over the corruption and the temptation to lose it or to run from your problem or to give in to the spirit that is in the world today. How is this possible when the very ones we are trying to touch are driving us crazy? Peter gives us the secret: We may "participate in the divine nature" (2 Pet. 1:4, NIV).

Participating in God's divine nature may sound far-out at first. But let me tell you, it is as practical and concrete as brushing your teeth in the morning.

Just as there are rules of etiquette and protocol in the natural life, there are standards of behavior in the spiritual life. The way we govern ourselves in our everyday lives speaks loudly to others about our upbringing, family and parents, and the kind of man or woman we have become.

When my three sons were under the age of three (yes, they're adopted), my husband and I started to teach them how to be gentlemen. We want them to learn how to love one another and to treat each other and their sisters with kindness so they will be good fathers.

When I see one of the boys grab the coveted toy tractor and bonk his brother on the head while the other clobbers him in the back with his sister's pink plastic purse, I keep telling myself that we have at least fifteen more years to work on "love one another." Then I wonder why they are playing with their sister's pink plastic purse!

Good manners are great; however, the protocol of the Holy Spirit is far above that. Jesus said, "You will know they are mine because they have love for each other" (see John 13:35). First, we must relinquish our right to have it our way. The Lord loves a tender, yielded heart that acknowledges that His way is best. When I'm defending my rights, ugly words pour out of my mouth. Those words are the fruit of anger and unforgiveness.

My husband reminds me that I occasionally have an anointing for thinking of something extremely sarcastic that can take the joy right out of "someone." Me? He must be thinking of someone else.

If there is an example in the Word of a woman who could be described as charming, it is the Proverbs 31 woman. For centuries she has been considered a paragon for women to emulate. But who can walk in perfection?

I want to share my thoughts and impressions, past and present, and the principles the Lord has taught me concerning character development. Then we can move on and forget about her.

## I Say She Was On Drugs

When I first began to study the account of the Proverbs 31 woman, I decided that she was either hyperactive with an extremely high metabolism or on some Old Testament version of amphetamines. I heard numerous teachings on this truly awesome woman. They were very discouraging, because I knew that I could never be like her.

Every Mother's Day, the guest speaker would have us turn to Proverbs 31, and I knew exactly where we were going. As soon as the text was announced, I was sure I heard hundreds of women, even those who had already died, begin to weep quietly as they said, "Please, not her again." Our beautiful corsages suddenly wilted on our new dresses.

The way she's described you figure she was at least as gorgeous as Christie Brinkley with that don't-hate-me-because-I'm-beautiful hair. And she was tall, very very tall — at least a foot taller than I am. She had a perfectly maintained year-round tan, a size two body and an immaculately kept house that had an original lid for each Tupperware bowl. She was Martha Stewart and Julia Child embodied in one woman.

Of course, her garden produced all organically grown food, and she had perfect children, servants, flocks and herds. Everyone in her family wore Laura Ashley garments made from the cotton she grew and spun and then hand-stenciled by the midnight oil.

And most important, the minister always reminded us, were her spiritual qualities. This saint was Kathryn Kuhlman, Marilyn Hickey, both Marys (Magdalene and the mother of Jesus) and Gloria Copeland all in one person.

One service that exalted the Proverbs 31 woman is particularly memorable. By the end of the sermon, the tiny flaw in my pantyhose had become a giant hole from mid-thigh to kneecap because I was picking at it with the pen I should have been taking notes with. A dull pain was beginning to move from my neck into my eyeball as we sang the closing chorus. The gentlemen in the audience gave the visiting minister a hearty "Amen," followed by a clapping ovation. I just wanted to go home.

## I'm Trying to Sit at His Feet, But Who's Going to Order the Take-out?

I was being oppressed by a dead woman. The demands of marriage, motherhood, ministry and money management keep me so busy that I cannot grow a garden, raise live-stock, knit blankets or fashion buffalo hide into shoes for my family.

If the truth be known, I do not grow things very well. My husband told me that once when we were shopping, I was eyeing a lovely ivy, and he heard it scream, "Please don't buy me lady, I want to live!" If a button falls off, the garment goes into the back of the closet, waiting for the day when I might purchase some thread and a little pack of needles. Abagael and Joshua's cribs are in our bedroom where we have a mixture of bathrobes, computers and baby stuff neatly strewn on dressers, on the floor and under the bed.

I studied this proverbial woman, endeavoring to make peace with her. The more I studied, the more I began to see that these few verses were not a description of her day but a description of her life.

King Solomon wrote this loving tribute to his mother, the famous Bathsheba. His words should be extremely encouraging to us. Bathsheba was a shattered, broken woman, one who had gambled everything in order to be loved. At the end of her life, her children rose up to bless her.

## Don't I Know You From Somewhere, Honey?

Have you ever had a problem with someone who insisted on not doing things your way, which of course is the right way? For years I tried to teach my husband the purpose of the clothes hamper. He said he understood, but I continued to find dirty socks and underwear wadded and tossed Michael Jordan style, in the direction of the hamper, but with little accuracy.

One day I decided I had had enough. Feeling like a martyr and very sorry for myself, I charged into the room where my unsuspecting husband sat and launched into a tirade that started out with dirty clothes and ended up with an incident that had taken place ten years earlier.

My stricken husband sat there looking at me as though I had lost my mind. When I came to myself, I couldn't believe what I was saying. All of a sudden it was not his problem anymore. It was my problem.

A lack of kindness and mercy are indications that we are still reactors when we need to be responders. One quality has to do with the flesh, the other with the spirit.

Some years ago the Lord drove home this principle — and its importance in my walk with Him as His ambassador. I was asked to sing once a month at the large church in Central Florida that I was attending. One Sunday afternoon I made a quick trip to the grocery store on the way home from church. While waiting in the checkout line, I felt a sharp pain on the back of my heels. I turned around to see an elderly couple. One of them had pushed a shopping cart into my feet, and he seemed oblivious to the pain he had caused. I was mad. Glaring at them, I opened my mouth to tell them off. Before I could utter a word, the precious little lady spoke: "You are the little girl who sings at church on Sundays, aren't you? You have been such a blessing to us. I know this meeting was ordained by the Lord so we could tell you how much you mean to us."

She was right. The meeting was ordained by God, but not for the reason she thought. As she and her husband shuffled out the door, she pressed a five-dollar bill into my hand. The amount was within pennies of my grocery bill. I could have died on the spot, except for the fact that I was not really crazy about facing the Master at that moment.

That valuable lesson has remained with me for fifteen years. Mercy is better than judgment.

## No One Cares How Much You Know 'Til They Know How Much You Care

We can have a tremendous amount of knowledge, an incredible understanding of the Word and revelation that will make people gasp with amazement, but if we lack mercy and compassion, who will listen?

We have all known men and women of God who had accurate and anointed gifts. When they opened their mouths, God's voice spoke. Yet, when you got to know them on a personal basis, it was obvious they lacked kindness. Either they never learned how to be nice, or pride in their God-given gifts caused them to forget that the desire of God's heart was for them to reach out and touch people.

### There Is a Beautiful Color Picture in Your Negative

Remember what Peter wrote: Everything we need for godliness has already been placed inside us (see 2 Pet. 1:3). It is not an automatic response. Peter goes on to say that this godly character must be actively developed. To develop literally means to unfold more completely.

> For this very reason, make every effort to add to your faith goodness; and to goodness, knowledge; and to knowledge, self-control; and to self-control, perseverance; and to perseverance, godliness; and to godliness, brotherly kindness; and to brotherly kindness, love. For if you possess these qualities in increasing measure, they will keep you from being ineffective and unproductive in your knowledge of our Lord Jesus Christ (2 Pet. 1:5-8, NIV).

It was always my mother's duty to teach me and my two brothers good manners. She wanted us to be able to go to the store, out to dinner or to our Sicilian relatives' homes

117

and not embarrass her by acting like little brats. (Thanks, Mom!)

A child is not born polite but must learn politeness by example and training so they will be a blessing and not an embarrassment to their parents. We who love our precious heavenly Father must also learn and be trained so that we might be a blessing and not an embarrassment to Him and His Kingdom.

The Holy Spirit, who teaches us and leads us into all truth, basically does the same thing in the spiritual realm as our mothers did in the natural.

I would like to share with you some of the rules of etiquette of the Holy Spirit that I have found in the previous scripture. I call them Christian graces.

## 1. Faith

We cannot please God without it and we are miserable company to be with when we don't exercise it.

## 2. Goodness

Goodness is moral excellence, which includes honesty, integrity, modesty and righteousness. It's not always the man who takes a second leering glance at an attractive woman anymore. Our society has made it acceptable behavior to make suggestive remarks to coworkers and watch questionable television shows. Some of us have even had conversations with our church friends that dishonor the name of Jesus. As a result, the church has been reaping the fruit from these seemingly innocent seeds. At the same time, the world mocks those with high morals and calls them old-fashioned. Young people who still blush are ridiculed. We need the Lord to restore our innocence.

## 3. Knowledge

Peter was not talking about the accumulation of facts or simply the memorization of God's word. He was talking about knowing God. One of the worst enemies to knowing God intimately is a complacency that steals our hunger for more of Him. Too many of us have a "been there, done that" attitude. The Lord has so much more for us. His desire is for us to reach out to Him.

## 4. Self-control

This next one gets stuck in my throat. Honesty demands that I reveal to you that I am still working on this one. The hand weights, the stack of Richard Simmon's videos, the bicycle, and the track (actually, Randi is responsible for that one) are dusty reminders of that fact.

In James 3 we are cautioned about the taming of the tongue. We are held responsible for the words we speak. Tame the tongue, and self-control will come a little easier.

## 5. Perseverance

This is the foundation of every promise that has or will come to pass. Waiting can create in you a bitter attitude that says, "I just can't stand this any longer. Why, God, why?" Or it can make you sweet. It was through faith and patience Abraham obtained the promise. Whatever you do, do not give up. You are almost there.

## 6. Godliness

This is not a holier-than-thou attitude. Nor is it an I-can-pray-longer-and-louder-than-you spirit. It doesn't have anything to do with big earrings, toenail polish, hemlines, how high I pile my hair on my head or how many pins shake out of my hair when the glory falls. Godliness has nothing to do with arguing over praise choruses versus the hymnal, the clerical collar versus the silk tie, or the collarless shirt buttoned up past your neck that is popular now but really makes you sweat.

Godliness is all those things that attract us to God — love, righteousness, holiness, kindness, forgiveness and patience.

## 7. Brotherly Kindness

There are times when the Holy Spirit will impress you to go out of your way to bless someone. It is usually at night, when you don't feel like it, when your house has a severe plumbing problem or when you are broke. A simple Yes, Lord, will bring you an eternal reward.

## 8. Love

It has been said that the body of Christ is the only body that will devour itself. We often shoot our wounded and are not very kind to each other.

Those are the Christian graces found in 2 Peter 1. The following are graces the Lord has pressed me into, born out of my need to relate to other — yes, you guessed it — difficult people!

Every time I respond to a difficult situation and resist the temptation to react according to my feelings, the flesh or the devil, something within me dies just a little more. The part that dies is the part that does not look like Jesus. Ah, but the part of me that lives, the gracious character of the Holy Spirit, brings the Father great joy, and it brings me great peace.

## 9. Instances or acts of kindness

How about sending a card to your pastor? It might say, "I really enjoyed your two-and-a-half-hour sermon last Sunday on the utensils from the Tabernacle." Or maybe send a $2.99 pre-packaged bunch of flowers from the Save-A-Lot-

120

of-Dough store for a friend. How about a kind word to a mate that says, "I appreciate how hard you work for me"? These small gestures say, "I was thinking about you today and wanted you to know how special you are to the Lord and to me." People listen a lot better to your message if your method is filled with love.

## 10. Humility

This is a quality of the heart that cannot be feigned. It is worked in us by continually remembering that we are the Master's friend — and His servant. "Let another's lips praise you and not your own."

## 11. Tolerance

I live in a household of snorers. My husband snores, my children snore and even my poodle snores. As I lay in bed at night, it's surround sound snoring. I put a pillow over my head and headphones over my ears and listen to praise tapes on my Walkman. I even tried listening to an R. W. Shambach tape at the highest volume. Still, stereo snoring. It is maddening. Grabbing a blanket and pillow, I have made a pilgrimage to the sofa, only to have my poodle follow me, curl up at my feet — and start snoring!

Not long after my intolerance had reached its limit I was away on a ministry trip. Settling into the hotel bed, I remember thinking, *Tonight I get to sleep the entire night through. No crying babies and no snoring.*

I awoke the next morning greatly refreshed. I looked over to see my mother, who had accompanied me, staring at me from the other bed. I said, "Praise God for a good night's rest! I slept well."

Her tight-lipped answer to me was, "Well, I didn't. You snore!" Tolerance is an excellent Christian grace. You sow to others what you need for yourself.

121

## 12. Hospitality and Fellowship

We live in a selfish society, and we have to resist the temptation to remain entirely focused on self. One way that is accomplished is by lending our time and attention to others.

I was once in the middle of a tremendous battle in my life, a battle of my mind and emotions. My pastor's wife, Dr. Jeana Tomlinson, called to inform me that she was coming to pick me up and that I was to be ready. I did not want to go; I wanted to stay home in my pajamas. However, knowing how busy she is, I realized this was a sacrifice for her. She took me to lunch and then shopping for some new clothes.

As we sat talking over lunch I said to her, "Jeana, I need a psychiatrist."

"No, you don't, you need a friend," she said. I got healed that day.

Hopefully, you have been reading this chapter with a yellow highlighter in hand, marking those places where the Spirit of God is showing you that a change is needed. Now I am not insinuating that *you* need help — I'm sure you're just making notes for someone else. Still, there is one more exciting thought that I would like to share.

## Reward

Charm schools exist to prepare you to attend social, business or family gatherings with grace and ease. Once you graduate, you can be at ease having high tea with the queen or a fish fry at the church with your "everyday" friends. You can do it all without fear of feeling out of place.

> For if these things [Christian graces] be in you, and abound, they make you that ye shall neither be barren nor unfruitful in the knowledge of our Lord

Jesus Christ. But he that lacketh these things is blind, and cannot see afar off, and hath forgotten that he was purged from his old sins (2 Pet. 1:8-9).

There is a reward for graduating from this charm school — not merely a certificate of completion but the promise of the abundance of fruit in every area of our lives. God can trust you. He can bring you before kings or behind prison walls, knowing you will be an ambassador of His grace and love and have the ear of the Holy Spirit to respond to people, especially the difficult ones.

Every great man and woman who was used by God to touch his or her generation, simply gave expression to his impression. Nations, cities and families were changed.

It's not always the rich or the mighty that He uses. He just seeks someone who is willing to be a blessing to bring hope, deliverance and help when it is needed the most.

Which one of these Christian graces touched you for Jesus? Who was it that God sent into your life wearing love-colored glasses when they looked at you? What one person, congregation, family member or prayer group stood for you, holding on and refusing to let go?

Someone was possessed by the love of God for you. Now it's your turn!

# 10

# Pardon Me, but I Need to Tell You This in Love

In the Word, relationship problems multiplied as fast as the earth's population. In Genesis alone, Adam and Eve, blaming each other and the serpent, refused to accept responsibility for their sin. In a fit of jealous anger, Cain murdered his brother Abel; Sarah abused and rejected her slave Hagar; Jacob stole Esau's birthright and fled in shame, running for his life. Laman cheated Jacob by giving him Leah for his wife instead of Rachel, and Joseph's jealous brothers sold him into slavery.

And what about the New Testament? Look at the way Jesus' disciples behaved toward one another. They were jealous, angry, always jockeying for a position of honor. The argument between Paul and Barnabas concerning Mark was so bad that their relationship ended.

Why are we so surprised when we have problems in our relationships with each other? To expect perfect relationships between ourselves and others is unrealistic.

One person describes Christian fellowship as coming together like grapes — crushed, with skins of ego broken, the ripe fragrant juices of life mingling together in the wine of sharing, understanding and caring. Yeah, right!

In fellowship with others, we receive support, encouragement, acceptance, help and love. But we also experience rejection, judgment, discouragement, insensitivity and jealousy.

If I expect to walk in right relationship with another, I have to have an open-arms approach to every person in my life regardless of the way he or she treats me.

Love is known by the action it takes. The New Testament does not concern itself with how we feel but with how we treat one another. We may not like the idea very much, but the Word tells us to forgive those who mistreat us.

When we let our emotions instead of our spirits determine our actions, we displease God. Our emotions are meant to enrich our lives, not direct them. Have you ever called yourself a hypocrite as you expressed forgiveness with your mouth but felt unforgiveness in your heart? Is it hypocritical to act contrary to our emotions?

We cannot feel our way to new actions, but we can act our way to new feelings.

Since love is known by actions, God will judge our love on the basis of how we treat the least important people in our lives. We can safely say that we do not love God any more than we love the least lovable person.

Here are some ways that indicate that we love ourselves more than we love our neighbors:

1. *Do we excuse our neighbors' behavior as graciously as we excuse our own?*

We're late for a meeting because we're so busy. Our neighbors are late because they are inconsiderate. We say unkind words because we had a bad day. Our neighbors say unkind words because they are thoughtless and uncaring people.

2. *Do we accept our neighbors' emotions as easily as we accept our own?*

We're depressed because of a difficult situation. Our friends are depressed because they indulge in self-pity. We have a right to be angry; they are just immature.

> Anyone who intends to come with me has to let me lead. You're not in the drivers' seat — I am. Don't run from suffering; embrace it. Follow me and I'll show you how. Self-help is no help at all. Self-sacrifice is the way, my way, to finding yourself, your true self (Luke 9:23-24, MSG).

3. *Do we defend the reputations of others as carefully as we defend our own?*

We would never expose all of our character flaws or, God forbid, our sins! However, we often do not hesitate to tell others about people who have sinned against, hurt or failed us.

I was at a restaurant with a group after a church service when the conversation turned to a well-known minister. People talked about the phenomenal services he was having and the way the favor of God was increasing on his life. Then someone at the table piped up, "Were any of you aware of the fact that he has been married before?" I failed to understand what purpose that comment had. Why is it we feel the need to share a negative word about a brother or sister in the Lord, especially when they are a great blessing to many?

4. *Do we forgive some as readily as we forgive others?*

If someone borrows a tape, a book, or a Tupperware bowl and forgets to return it, do we withhold forgiveness? I have an entire cupboard of Tupperware I don't recall purchasing. As a matter of fact, I have no idea where all these containers came from and often joke about it. However, I'm sure Mrs. Anita Life doesn't think it's very cute when she has nowhere to put her leftover Jell-O salad.

5. *Do we anticipate and meet the needs of others in the same manner that we desire for our needs to be anticipated and met?*

We have often heard that actions speak louder than words. My six favorite words are, "What can I do to help?" — not "Oh, gee, I really love you!"

## I Gotta Be Me

That was the slogan of the youth of the sixties and seventies, the generation that lived for the *now*. They lived for themselves and denied themselves nothing. They produced fatherless children and dysfunctional families; drugs and alcohol dulled the pain of their hurting, lonely lives.

Jesus told us that by denying ourselves, we could have the life we desire. But we usually do just the opposite. Here is a simple description of those attitudes that are opposed to self-denial.

*Self-importance.* If we walk into a gathering wondering how many people are going to speak to us, who will notice us, who remembered our important prayer requests or when our birthdays are, we are choosing self-importance. We should welcome the lonely, be a friend to the friendless, listen to the ignored, hug those who are hurting and pray for the discouraged.

*Self-occupation.* If we arrive at a gathering with a list of special people we want to see or things we must do, we may be so self-occupied that we ignore the hurting people around us. The way to avoid self-occupation is to lay down our plans long enough to meet the needs of others. Too often we help people only when we are free to choose the time and the place and the way we are going to do it. Unfortunately, people need help when we have made previous plans. Randi and I postpone any chance of retirement every time we take a new baby into our home. Right now, it looks as though we will be 101 before the kids leave home and we can retire.

*Self-affection.* If we talk about our achievements, our families and our problems at the expense of others, we allow self-affection to run our lives. How well do you listen? Do you often listen so that you can turn the conversation back to yourself, or do you really listen to what someone is saying?

*Self-protection.* Our egos want to defend themselves against criticism and correction. If we can avoid self-protection, we will be able to receive criticism or correction without putting down those who correct us: "The way she treats her husband. How dare she tell me how to treat *mine?*" We place ourselves above correction when we say such things as, "I won't listen to anything spoken in that harsh spirit."

*Self-inspection.* Some people check their feelings to see if they should go to church, read the Word or clean the house. That's self-inspection. We think it is the discerning of spirits! God has called us to walk in obedience to His Word and His Spirit, not in obedience to our feelings.

*Self-sufficiency.* Whether we like it or not, God has commanded an interdependent lifestyle for believers. Some people are great givers, but it is very difficult for them to receive from others. One way to prevent self-sufficiency is to admit that we need others and that we don't have it all together.

Who is the least lovable person in your life? Remind

yourself that you don't love God any more than you love that person.

> Jesus said "Love the Lord your God with all your passion and prayer and intelligence." This is the most important, the first on any list. But there is a second to set alongside it: "Love others as well as you love yourself." These two commandments are pegs; everything from God's Law and the Prophets hangs from them (Matt. 22:37-40, MSG).

## You Are a One-of-a-Kind Original

We are original masterpieces created by the Master of the universe. Because we bear His image, God has given us a place of dominion. When we dishonor other people, we dishonor God.

Even the members of the Godhead give honor to one another. The Father glorifies Jesus (John 17:24). Jesus seeks to glorify the Father (John 14:13; 17:4). The Holy Spirit glorifies the Father and Jesus (John 15:26; 16:14).

Our society has lost the concept of honoring one another. In Gary Smalley's video on the subject of honor, he passes a violin around the room. When it is about halfway through the audience, Smalley announces that the violin is a priceless Stradivarius. "Aahh," each persons uttered, passing the violin to the next person more carefully. Smalley made his point: The true meaning of "to honor" is to *Aahh!*

Christians have allowed society to lose a true understanding of the word *respect*. When the rebels of the sixties discarded manners, and the radicals of the seventies and eighties demanded that all distinctions between men and women be erased, some Christians joined the ranks.

Christian men and children stopped standing when women entered the room and no longer held doors open for them. Children were often not taught to respect their elders. The gift of hospitality is rarely practiced because we are too busy, and the supreme act of humbly confessing our sins to one another is almost obsolete.

You can demonstrate honor to someone by approaching them and not waiting for them to come to you. Embrace them with your eyes; welcome them with a hug or a handshake. Demonstrate honor and acceptance with a smile, eye contact and a pleasant tone of voice.

I don't like it when someone looks past me while I'm talking to them or shaking his or her hand. I know the person is waiting for me to shut up and move out of the way. It gives me the feeling that I am not as important as they are — or as the person they are *really* waiting to talk to.

> If one gives answer before he hears, it is his folly and shame (Prov. 18:13, RSV).

> My dear brothers, take note of this: Everyone should be quick to listen, slow to speak and slow to become angry (James 1:19, NIV).

Sometimes I find myself listening with an answer already in my head instead of listening in order to really hear what is being said. And I've been on the receiving end of that kind of behavior as well. At times I have expressed a fear or a problem I was struggling with and gotten a cliché answer such as: "It's obvious you're not trusting in the Lord" — just before I got hit with the person's big black Bible!

Talkative people utter about twelve thousand sentences a day. That averages out to about one hundred thousand words.

## Pardon Me, but I Need to Tell You This in Love

If we encourage honor and treat others as we want to be treated, our relationship problems will be few. But what if you do have a problem with another person? How do you handle it? Do you confront the person, avoid her, talk about her to a third party, or forgive and forget?

Because many of us, myself included, avoid confrontations at all costs, we often end up discussing problems with the wrong person.

Gossip is the number one relationship problem in the church today. Gossip is the passing on of negative information about someone not present. Just gather two or three people together in an office or a prayer meeting, and it won't be long before we disappoint, anger, hurt or frustrate one another. We talk to others about those who have displeased us. We gossip. Gossip in turn sows seeds of distrust, and we end up having a bad attitude toward those we should love.

Gossip is less threatening than talking face-to-face with the problem person. We often use gossip to reinforce our own image at the expense of destroying the images of others.

Many of us have had someone we thought was our friend share negative things with another person we also considered a friend. When the negative report came back to us, it crushed us.

Gossip gives us power. We can use it to manipulate people and to bring about a desired change. We can also drum up sympathy for ourselves by telling others about the awful way we have been treated.

Suppose Mary Jones worked in the church nursery with me on Sunday, and all she did was sit in a rocking chair and yak with the mothers. In my frustration, I tell you about Mary's lack of initiative. So the next month when it is your turn to work in the nursery with her, you see Mary through the negative words I spoke.

What do we do with Mary Jones? She feels working in the nursery is her ministry. She can't sing, so that leaves out choir ministry.

The Word is very clear about rebuking people who are in sin (Matt. 18:15-17). But Mary was not in sin. She was just thoughtless. Do we speak to her? Where do grace and forgiveness fit into the picture?

Learning when a person is in sin or when he just has a personality problem that we need to overlook requires prayer and wisdom from the Lord.

When are you more likely to change? — when you are criticized, or when you are accepted and loved in spite of your failures?

What about Mary Jones' irresponsible attitude toward nursery duty? Her actions are not sinful. You now have an opportunity to grow in grace and give Mary what she does not deserve — unconditional forgiveness and complete acceptance. If you choose this route, you are also deciding to never mention her behavior to anyone else.

Jesus sharply rebuked anyone who sinned against God and led others into sin. But He never defended Himself against personal attack.

If we compare the number of times the Word tells us to rebuke with the number of times we are told to love one another, we will see that the emphasis is on unconditional love.

## How, When and Where

If you are in a situation in which something *must* be said, confrontation is the only option. It is wise to choose the time, the place and your words prayerfully. Most of us let problems pile up until we have a big blowout with someone. Then we wind up confronting the person in a way that is so hurtful that the other person can't hear what you are saying.

**You:** Pastor Blabbershoot, your sermons are so boring. Your hairpiece looks as if a squirrel died on your head, and you are so fat the elders are widening your office door. There, I feel so much better. How about you?

**Pastor Blabbershoot:** (lying on the floor in his collarless shirt that the Women's Ministry gave him for Christmas) AAGGHH!

Our words need to be non-inflammatory and our voice calm, sweet and free of accusation and judgment. We need to go to the person with a fresh awareness of our own need for the continual flow of God's grace and mercy in our lives.

And so we approach Mary:

**You:** Mary, I'm so sick and tired of doing all the work while you sit there on your blessed assurance, drinking soda and eating the children's snacks.

Instead it should go like this:

**You:** Mary, I'm feeling a little overwhelmed at the moment. Suzie has one finger in the light socket and the other up baby Eggbert's nose. And he has a cold. Could you please help me?

What are my motives? Do I have the other person's best interests at heart, or do I just want them to straighten out because they annoy me? If I can't correct in love, I shouldn't speak.

Is this an opportunity to forgive others as God forgives me, or is the problem my judgmental attitude rather than the person's behavior? If it is my attitude, I won't speak.

Having many children as well as extra people in my house, I have learned a few principles about how to speak the truth in love without completely destroying the person I'm talking to. I try not to criticize his or her past behavior, but speak what you want to see happen.

**You:** Mary, I hate to pull you away from your friends, but I'm really weary and need help. Could you take over for me now?

Remember, gossip destroys fellowship. Correction gains more favor than flattery. Let's speak the truth in love, knowing that we cannot protect people from pain.

I myself am convinced, my brothers, that you yourselves are full of goodness, complete in knowledge and competent to instruct one another (Rom. 15:14, NIV).

## Handling Correction

How do you handle criticism and correction? When we have wronged others, we should go to them to seek restoration and not exoneration. If we want them to tell us that we're still OK, that we are excused, that it really wasn't that big a deal, then we are seeking exoneration. That's when we bypass the problem, avoid talking about it and think only about clearing our names. We may say "I'm sorry," but flippantly.

Exoneration, like making up, is external. Restoration, on the other hand, is internal and brings healing. It centers on the relationship between two people and the harm done to it by one's thoughtlessness or sin. The offender comes in humility to say, "I was wrong. I've hurt you, and I need you to forgive me."

If we are criticized, our natural reaction is to counterattack and put the other person on the defensive. We say: "That's not true," or "You don't understand," or "You're wrong."

Self screams against being put down. It demands to be heard. It is only through prayer and the power of the Holy Spirit that we remain humble and non-defensive. When we can really listen to those who are angry with us and ask to be forgiven and restored, then we care more about our relationship's being right than just about being right ourselves.

Remember to respond to the part of the accusation that is true for you. Then flop down, open a large barrel of animal cookies or a box of Godiva chocolates (my favorite comfort food) and wash it all down with Eggbert's bottle!

# 11

# Ruth, You Are Getting on My Nerves. Love, Naomi

Have you ever had a friend who absolutely drove you crazy? You're discouraged, and you pour your heart out. What does she do? She sits there patting your hand and is so cheerful you want to throw up. That's not what you needed her for. You didn't want encouragement — you wanted her to pat you on the back and give you lots of sympathy and compassion. Everyone needs compassion. And don't forget pity. We need lots of pity.

I found out that when you have a friend who is always happy and excited, it's frustrating to be pitiful and miserable all by yourself. I much prefer to have my friends deeply affected by my misery and order me large quantities of pizza. Statistics have proven that pizza with the built-in cheese crust rates high up there on the list of comfort foods, followed closely by Reese's Peanut Butter Cups.

Maybe you have a friend like one of my distant relatives. When I poured out my heart to her, she listened quietly and patiently — until I took a breath in mid-sentence. Before I could go on, she proceeded to inform me that she too had experienced the exact same pain or problem. Of course, hers was far more serious or painful than mine could ever have been.

In frustration, I tried to trick her by telling her that I had been bitten recently by a wombat and asked if she would please pray for me. This led her to tell me a story from her childhood. During a delicious poultry dinner, she told her family that her pet chicken was missing. As furtive glances were exchanged across the table, the innocent little eight-year-old girl realized that she was eating her best friend. Seventy-five years later, this incident still brought tears to her eyes. So much for my wombat bite.

## We're Not in Kansas Anymore, Toto

And so it was with Naomi. She was pitiful, and what's worse, there was not a Pizza Hut in sight.

Naomi married a man by the name of Elimelech, and they settled in the town of Bethlehem. There was a famine in the land, and although they had property there they felt forced to leave so that Elimelech could find work to support his growing family. They packed up their belongings, and along with their two sons Mahlon and Chilion (and you thought your name was awful), moved to a place called Moab.

In time the boys grew up and married Moabite women. Their choices of wives were not great from the point of view of compatibility; the Moabites worshiped false gods.

Going from bad to worse, Naomi not only lost her husband to a premature death but both of her sons as well. She found herself a widow and childless — a seemingly hopeless condition.

136

With great sorrow, Naomi packed up her meager belongings and prepared to return home to Bethlehem. She heard that God had blessed the area, and there was now plenty of everything. Family obligations dictated that her two widowed daughters-in-law also accompany her back home. However, she released them and with great sadness gave them permission to stay in Moab with their families and friends.

## Moving Time Again?

Naomi must have been a really cool mother-in-law, because neither one of her son's wives said, "Great, I'm out of here. It was nice knowing you, and if you ever come back to Moab, let's do lunch."

Instead, these girls began to weep and insisted that they go with her to Bethlehem. As they started out, Naomi again appealed to them. She wanted them to realize that there was absolutely no future for them if they went with her and that she loved them far too much to see them waste their futures.

In this beautiful story, I see Naomi full of pity and sorrow. She assumed that God had turned His hand against her, and as far as she was concerned there was absolutely nothing for her to do except go home and die.

In love and mercy, God sent Ruth to Naomi. However, Ruth wasn't just a pawn in this play. Her faithfulness to stay by Naomi's side brought her into God's destiny for her as well. In short, God gave Naomi a friend.

As much as I chafe when a friend tries to encourage me out of my misery, I realize the value of having wonderful friends, and I do have several. These are people who are real with me, not the type of people you often meet in Christian circles. There are many Christian women who cannot sustain any type of meaningful relationship with another Christian. Those relationships are superficial.

When we are asked in church on Sunday morning, "How are you doing?" we say, "You would not believe how incredibly blessed I am. I shine with the glory that radiates from the throne into my eyes!" Of course, we conveniently leave out the details of the near-fatal stabbing incident we had with our son before church that morning.

We don't always tell the whole truth because we know people who fellowship only around their problems, and we do not want to become like them. They are the ones with whom you avoid eye contact so you do not have to hear about their latest bout with intestinal flu. We so desire to maintain a positive confession that we get to the point of lying to everyone who genuinely cares about us, fearing that we might grieve the Holy Spirit if we tell the truth.

A newly-saved woman working in my office cut her finger on a postage machine. The wound was pretty deep, and it was bleeding profusely. All through the day others would ask, "How's your finger?" She would hold up her swollen, bloody finger and proclaim, "My finger is not cut, and I am not bleeding." Everybody thought she was a nut.

The Word of God does not say, "Calls things that *are* as though they were *not.*" It says, "Calls things that are not as though they were" (Rom. 4:17, NIV). The apostle Paul *acknowledged* the negative things, yet used his faith in the Lord as a battering ram to crash through the negatives to declared victory. He claimed that, as Christians, we are "As unknown, and yet well known; as dying, and, behold we live; as chastened, and not killed; As sorrowful, yet always rejoicing; as poor, yet making many rich; as having nothing, and yet possessing all things" (2 Cor. 6:9-10).

My employee's faith, though genuine, was misplaced. She should have said, "I know this looks pretty bad, but I know the Lord has already touched me." If the accident had happened to me, I would have hollered in pain and prayed for healing on the way to the Dairy Queen.

## Will You Be My Friend?

When my daughter Jerusha was a little girl, Randi and I were traveling as evangelists. Every week we were in a different church. I would try to find a few girls her age for her to play with at each place we had meetings. Of course, we were in one place only for a short time, and then the process would begin again.

When she was old enough to go to kindergarten, we settled in Winter Haven, Florida. I rejoiced, because now my little girl would have a normal life with real friends.

When I picked her up from school one day, I overheard her asking several little girls on the playground if she could be their friend. "No," said one of the ugliest little children I have ever seen. "You cannot be our friend. We already have friends. Go away." Needless to say, it nearly broke my heart, and I could not hold back the tears as I saw my precious little daughter hang her head and walk away. I wanted to shield her from the pain that people would intentionally or unintentionally inflict on her for the rest of her life.

Today she is nineteen years old, and her social life is far better than mine. Her phone rings off the hook. People have told me they are impressed with her trustworthiness and her ability to reach out to the shy, the hurting and especially the friendless, with a godly love. Where did she learn that? Where did that capacity to love and recognize the wounds of others come from? She remembered what it felt like to be friendless, and through the power of the Holy Spirit she became a friend to others.

We need to remember that person who reached out to us when we felt so very alone. Many times we put up a wall to protect us from intimacy because we remember what happened the last time we opened our hearts to someone and were betrayed or hurt.

## The Price of Being a Friend

"Friends come and friends go, but a true friend sticks by you like family" (Prov. 18:24, MSG). It's one thing to find a friend but another to keep that friendship strong and healthy. Many marriages and relationships falter because one person is expected to do all the giving. Cultivating a friend is like cultivating a crop: You reap what you sow.

Once the seed of friendship is sown, it must be tended. How? We water that seed through intercessory prayer. We weed it by removing from our hearts and minds any judgmental thoughts, hurt feelings, jealousy, mistrust or animosity. In order to have a friend, we need to be the kind of friend we want for ourselves.

One morning my husband and I were having a sort-of discussion. I knew what the problem was. He simply didn't understand that my idea was — I modestly admit — brilliant, and his idea was ridiculous. I know that most of you can sympathize with me. He left for the office without so much as a good-bye kiss. I was so angry I began to talk to myself in the bedroom. "I'm so sick and tired of...it's not fair...if God doesn't judge him He will have to apologize to Sodom and Gomorrah..."

In the midst of all this murmuring and complaining, I began to throw bed pillows on the floor. Suddenly another brilliant idea popped into my head. I decided that I would make only my side of the bed. I was amazed at the cleverness of my revenge. I began straightening only my side of the room. I cleared the cups and glasses off *my* nightstand, leaving his nightstand a mess.

Then I arranged all the pillow shams, European pillows and toss pillows (I have lots of them on my bed), leaving his side of the bed unmade and messy. As I stood back to admire my work, the Holy Spirit within me spoke quietly. "Cathy, are you pleased with yourself?"

Sitting on the floor, I began to weep. What was I sowing into my relationship? A spirit of division, separation, revenge and anger. I knew then that whatever I sowed that day in anger, I would have to reap in several crops of strife in my marriage and in my home.

Many times we do not see the need to invest ourselves in our own homes. Developing friendships with the people we live with can sure change the atmospheres of our homes. The apostle Peter reminded the Christian husband that it was vitally important for him to sow honor upon his Christian wife so that his prayers would not be hindered (see 1 Pet. 3:7). The Christian wife is to sow submission even to the non-Christian husband, for submission has the power to win him over (see 1 Pet. 3:1).

So what did I do? I lovingly changed the sheets, making sure I used the soft blue ones that are his favorite.

I don't always pass the test. In fact, I was about twenty minutes late in yielding to the Holy Spirit, but I continually strive to do better.

We need friends who will sharpen us. "The wounds from a lover are worth it; kisses from an enemy do you in" (Prov. 27:6, MSG). Watch out for those who always praise you. If all we hear is that everything we do is wonderful, we will never improve.

Notice that this verse says that the wounds inflicted upon us by a friend are worthwhile. Why would a friend wound you? Hopefully, because that friend is honest and wants what is best for you. He might tell you that you've been ministering to people for hours with pieces of salad stuck in your teeth. (And you wondered why everyone you prayed for was full of the joy of the Lord and laughed a lot.) Love is kind, but it is honest. It doesn't excuse wrongdoing just to keep someone happy and spare his feelings.

God is love. Have you ever felt the chastising end of His staff? It's a rod, sweetheart. Growth is painful. Becoming a man or woman of God and developing maturity requires discipline and correction. "In the end, serious reprimand is appreciated far more than bootlicking flattery" (Prov. 28:23, MSG).

When a friend, husband, wife or teacher counsels us, it may not be pleasant at that precise moment. However, the counsel, if it is well-founded, will motivate us to move in the right direction and help us succeed.

## Lean On Me...But Not Too Hard Until You Lose That Last Fifteen Pounds

A friend is a great support. Don't worry if you don't have a lot of them. Friends are like salt — a little goes a long way. Jesus didn't have a large number of close friends. Out of the twelve disciples, only three were really close to Him — Peter, James and John. Of the three, John was His closest friend.

I believe someone who has to have lots and lots of friends is insecure. That person has no confidence in himself, so he has to depend on the support and approval of others.

Have you ever been in the company of a name-dropper? I have, and I was not impressed. I sat through an entire lunch with a lady who named one well-known Christian after another. They all loved and needed her. While she was rattling on, I thought to myself, *If this lady knows all these famous people, what is she doing sitting in this crummy little restaurant with me?*

The people you fellowship with are an end-time prophecy of what you are going to be.

Don't hang out with angry people;

don't keep company with hotheads.
Bad temper is contagious —
don't get infected (Prov. 22:24-25, MSG).

Often someone, even a Christian, can be full of bitterness. The love of God may seem to draw you to them in an attempt to help. But the Bible warns us to keep up our defenses. Be sure not to become too involved with an angry, bitter man. People who are bitter have a tendency to spill out the bitterness of their heart on whoever will listen. They will tell you how badly they are being mistreated or how badly they were treated in the *last* church they attended.

It won't be long before you'll become infected. Unconsciously, you will find yourself relating to the negative attitude and outlook. When you sense that danger, break the relationship. "Can two walk together, except they be agreed?" (Amos 3:3). The Hebrew here denotes fellowship, and agreement means a connecting of souls through the Spirit. Don't allow yourself to be drawn into another's despondency or pessimism. Be warned — that is a *spirit!* You will lose your ability to minister to the other person. "Keep a sharp eye out for weeds of bitter discontent. A thistle or two gone to seed can ruin a whole garden in no time" (Heb. 12:15, MSG).

## Noble? Who, Me?

What a compliment — to be known as a man or woman of excellence. Boaz paid the highest compliment to Naomi's daughter-in-law, Ruth, when he said to her, "And now, my daughter, do not fear. I will do for you whatever you ask, for all my people in the city know that you are a woman of excellence" (Ruth 3:11, NAS).

What was it about Ruth that commanded such high praise from a man who was not even from the same country? I wonder if that praise could have come as a result of her faithful and loyal friendship to her mother-in-law.

Friendship will often cost you something. For Ruth, it was an expensive choice. She gave up her family, friends, land, security and everything that was her future. However, what she received in return did not compare to what she gave up.

Some years ago I found myself in the middle of hurt, anger, bewilderment, frustration and devastation in my marriage. I looked at my husband and yelled, "If you don't love me anymore, just divorce me." With equal emotion he yelled back, "I do love you, and divorce is not an option."

I have thought of that conversation many times through the years. I know people today who have gotten a divorce for little or no reason. And I am not referring only to divorce in marriage, but also to "divorce" within a church family, divorce between pastors and their congregations, and divorce between fathers and sons or mothers and daughters as well. Divorce seems to be easier than facing the issue. No one wants to change. How it must break our Father's heart!

One decision Randi and I made seemed like such a good idea at the time. We were pastoring, and we needed a children's pastor. My precious brother Steve was the most gifted children's pastor we knew, so we brought him out to serve with us. A year after his arrival, the church suffered a horrible split; I don't even remember the issues anymore. Isn't that the way it almost always is?

My sweet brother and I, who were inseparable as children, were now separated by the church. During that heartbreaking time, my parents drove up from Florida to be with us for Christmas. I spent much of the two weeks they were with us trying to convince them, pretty self-righteously, of *my* side of the story.

My parents were forced to spend two nights at a time

with each of their children. When I found out they were going to spend Christmas morning with my brother, I spewed hurtful, angry words at my mother. Without saying a word, she walked out of the room. Following her, I heard her crying, "Cathy, please don't do this to us. How can I choose between two children that I love equally with all of my life?"

It's a wonder that my parents love me the way they do and spend so much time with me.

> In Christ's family there can be no division into Jew and non-Jew, slave and free, male and female. Among us you are all equal. That is, we are all in common relationship with Jesus Christ (Gal. 3:28, MSG).

The Holy Spirit is the great superglue given by God to bring us all together in Christ Jesus. We can't expect the Father to choose sides.

When I realized what I had done, I cried out to the Lord for mercy. Thankfully He healed me of temporary idiot's disease, and my sweet brother and I walk together in fellowship again. A friend loveth at all times!

# 12

# Looking for Love
# in All the Wrong Places

Recently I returned from a ministry conference where there was a tremendous move of the Spirit of God. I came home just in time to face a medical crisis involving one of our children. On top of that, I was battling severe bronchitis as well as dealing with a myriad of ministry and home-life pressures all by myself because my husband was in Latvia.

One day during that time I decided I had had it. Being tired, totally stressed out and missing my solid quality time in the Word and prayer, I retreated to a bubble bath. Bad move.

When you are really tired and weary from the battle, do not, under any circumstances, take off your clothes and stand naked before a full-length mirror.

I could feel myself starting to faint as I realized that I

looked like my eighty-eight-year-old great-aunt Minnie, who had passed away five years before.

My eldest daughter, Jerusha, rescued me and dragged me into the family room (after I donned a bathrobe), announcing that we were going to watch a movie. It was *First Knight*, a love story about Camelot. I watched the movie with absolute awe. Here was a beautiful young woman, passionately loved by two men — count them — *two* perfect men: first, Sean Connery, the king, who worshiped Guinevere, and then the young and restless Richard Gere. I sat there in my ratty old pink bathrobe, sighing and looking like my deceased great-aunt Minnie.

The enemy was setting me up. He was using my tiredness, my loneliness, an infirmity and the hormones that come to life every month to tempt me to compare myself to this beautiful young starlet. It didn't matter that the movie was just a fable. I compared it to my life and decided that my life stunk. Oh, to be so desired, to have long thick hair that is still beautiful even after plunging down a hundred-foot waterfall. To be...loved!

That, my dear friend, is Satan's biggest lie of this century. He tells you that everyone is smarter than you, that all the other women are goddesses compared to you and that most people are happier, godlier, more loved and more appreciated than you are.

What starts out as a twinge of discouragement evolves into thoughts of hopelessness. If you continue down that path, depression, despair and apathy are not far away. Slowly your passion for Jesus wanes. One day you realize you are not in the same place with the Holy Spirit as you once were. When I reach that point, I run back into the arms of Jesus, because I know the consequences of crossing the line. When you are bored, frustrated, not studying the Word and praying, you become vulnerable to any temptation the enemy wants to throw at you.

## The Moment You Step Into Confusion, You Lose Your Grip

Spring was in the air, and the battles were on. (I have absolutely no idea whatsoever why battles were scheduled in the spring.) Second Samuel 11 tells us that David sent Joab, his commanding officer, out to besiege some people, and King David stayed home. That would have been all right, except that traditionally kings went to battle with their men.

So here we see David hanging around his house, being set up by the enemy because he was not where he was supposed to be. That was his first mistake. He should have been out with his men besieging people. He was in the wrong place.

David was a man of blood and war and never turned down a chance for a good rumble. But the battles held no interest for him this time. He became bored and restless, and the stage was set against this man who had been described as a man after God's own heart. Somehow and somewhere David lost his psalmist's passion for God.

On a warm spring night, he rose up from his bed and took a walk on the roof.

## Don't Buy the Lie

A few hundred yards from the palace, a beautiful young woman was experiencing her own crisis. Just as the enemy was setting up David, he was equally ruthless with Bathsheba. Her husband, Uriah, was gone, and she couldn't sleep. She knew she came in second to Uriah's career. He was a loyal soldier to the king. *If we have a child together, things will be different,* Bathsheba may have speculated. But when your husband is a zealot and a workaholic who is married to the military, babies are a problem.

Bathsheba knew she was a beautiful woman. Men always

148

looked hard and long when she was at the market or at the house of worship. It seemed a cruel fate that she was married to a man who was never there to appreciate her beauty.

*Perhaps a nice bath would relax me and help me to sleep,* she thought. It was a night she would remember as long as she lived.

There is something that I have never understood about rooftop bathing. If you are in a rooftop Jacuzzi, and there are many rooftops higher than yours, does it ever occur to you that you just might be seen?

King David rounded the corner just in time to see Bathsheba emerge from her bubble bath, and he got a good glimpse of this gorgeous woman. That was all he needed. The trap was sprung.

A sharp knock on Bathsheba's door soon aroused her household, and Bathsheba heard the words of King David's servant. The great king was summoning her to the palace. She knew instinctively what he wanted, and the feeling made her heart beat faster. She was starved for affection, and now the king wanted her. There is a certain excitement and exhilaration that comes to the pursued, however fleeting though it may be.

My father and I have a sharp difference of opinion concerning what happened next. He believes that upon being summoned by the king, she had no recourse except to obey. I, on the other hand, have a totally different perspective of what could have happened in those chambers. David, for all his shortcomings, did have a heart for God. He knew and understood Jewish law and realized that a married woman was now standing in front of him. He was well aware that sin was crouching at his door and that its desire was to have him.

Bathsheba also knew the laws of God and, like her predecessor Abigail, she could have fallen on her face in front of David and cried, "Let not my Lord, I pray you, as the

149

Lord lives and as you live, seek to do evil in His sight." She could have gone right to his heart and to his relationship with God, but she did not. I believe that if King David had heard those words of truth from Bathsheba — realizing what he had almost done — he would have sent her home. When Abigail used David's relationship with God to appeal to him to change his mind, he did (see 1 Sam. 25).

As king, all David had to do was speak the word, and his desire was fulfilled. How different this man was compared to the young man who once mourned before God simply because he had cut a piece of robe from his enemy, King Saul!

When we believe that our wealth, position or anointing will keep us from the *big* sins, Satan lays out a trap for us. Behind every backsliding, every lost anointing and every moral failure, there is pride. "When pride cometh, then cometh shame: but with the lowly is wisdom" (Prov. 11:2).

Bathsheba was in a vulnerable state. This was her chance to receive the adoration, the flattery of his desire and the love she so desperately wanted.

God has created us to be loved, nurtured and honored. I need to be cuddled and often will ask my husband just to put his arms around me and hold me. I get annoyed when he holds me with one arm while he moves my head around, jockeying for a position so he can also watch TV. Does that ever happen to you?

I believe that Bathsheba was flattered. I can see her preparing to go before the king. Her hair had to look just right, and she would use the perfume that her husband never seemed to notice. This was not simply a sexual thing for her, as it was for David. She had been summoned by no ordinary man. He was the king! And he wanted *her*. He found her attractive and desirable. He sent for "poor, lonely Bathsheba."

## Uh, Oh! The Rabbit Died

After Bathsheba and David committed adultery, Bathsheba purified herself according to Jewish law before returning home. Doesn't that beat all? The word says that sin satisfies for a season. Evidently the satisfaction did not satisfy for very long.

The greater the level of honor and anointing that God entrusts to a man or woman, the less margin for error there is (see Luke 12:48). After this short affair was almost out of David's heart and mind, word came to him that Bathsheba was pregnant with his child. What did our great Bible hero do?

Twice he enticed her husband to come home from battle to be with his wife. Once, he went so far as to get the poor unsuspecting man drunk. Uriah's sense of duty to his country and comrades kept him from going to Bathsheba. Surely his love and duty must have shamed King David. God was giving David a chance to repent by frustrating all his schemes to wrangle out of the mess without actually humbling himself.

For years we have centered on David's moral failure and the result of it in his life. But what about Bathsheba? Rejection upon rejection — the man she had given herself to because of the hurt and rejection in her marriage was now dumping her to cover up what he did.

As small children in Sunday school, we sang a little chorus that said, "Be careful little eyes what you see. Be careful little mind what you think." I can grasp the truth in those words and understand their meaning better now that I am grown.

Before David ever saw Bathsheba bathing on that rooftop, the seeds of sin were already in his mind. When he saw her, he simply acted on something that was already there. Maybe he was in a midlife crisis or something. But I don't

151

ever remember learning that a midlife crisis is an acceptable reason for going off the deep end!

David then became a conspirator to murder. Desperate to come up with a way to redeem himself, he devised a plan for Uriah to be killed in action. David married Bathsheba and brought her to the palace. All's well that ends well, right? Not!

## The Prophet Tells It Like It Is

At the appointed time, just when it seemed as though David's plotting and planning had finally brought closure and relief, the prophet came on the scene. Nathan was not afraid of David, David's position or his wealth. The prophet was on assignment from God.

> Nathan said to David, "You are the man. Thus says the Lord, the God of Israel, 'I anointed you king over Israel, and I delivered you out of the hand of Saul; and I gave you your master's house, and your master's wives into your bosom, and gave you the house of Israel and of Judah; and if this were too little, I would add to you as much more (2 Sam. 12:7-8, RSV).

I wept when I read that verse. It is the sound of my Father's voice, in sorrow over one of His best-loved sons. Something was lost that day. Pain pierced David, not only because of the suffering he had brought upon innocent and undeserving lives, but also because he had broken the heart of his best friend, the One who had loved, honored and kept him all of his life.

David would soon experience the sorrow that was coming to his house as a result of sin — the death of four of his own sons before their time, the rape of his daughter by his son. I have never counseled or spoken to any person who

152

has told me that his sin was worth the price he ultimately paid.

## Whisperers, Gossips and Rejection

Bathsheba would share in a sorrow of a different kind. After completing the period of mourning for her husband, she was brought to the palace to become another wife for the king.

We can only imagine what life in the palace must have been like for Bathsheba. Having to walk around a place where the others there, from priest to prophet, wine-tasters to wives and those who hid in the shadows, whispered as she passed by must have increased her suffering greatly.

## I've Got a Secret — Or Do I?

A lot of people in the palace knew exactly what was going on. There were all the other wives, those who waited on David and Bathsheba when she was in the palace, and the officers who had arranged Uriah's little "accident" in battle. The Lord always lets someone know.

And do you think that they kept it a secret? No more than when someone tells you, "I want to tell you something, but promise me you won't tell anyone else. This is just between us." Usually, that means you are one of many they have already told.

Indiscretion with our secrets is part of the awful price we pay for a momentary lack of restraint. You never know who has told whom, who knows and how much they know. Do they know the real truth or the elaboration of the truth that has been passed on to them through who knows how many mouths? And when you are in ministry, being the betrayed or the betrayer causes years of distrust from others. Have you ever walked into a room and all of a sudden it becomes very quiet? You know by the look on each face that you were the topic of conversation. I imagine that must have happened to Bathsheba often.

All Bathsheba ever wanted was to be happy. Isn't that what is inside most of us? Singles tell me, "If I could just find a mate, then I'd really be happy." I have heard married people say, "If I could just get rid of the mate I have and get another one, my happiness would be complete." They live under an illusion. Even in the very best of Christian marriages, both partners will tell you that you have to work at it. The enemy is out to destroy those who will listen to his lies.

If you are looking for a relationship to make you deliriously happy you will be disappointed, because the reality is never as great as the expectation.

Being rejected by two men that she had loved and now being subjected to the unkind and hurtful remarks of certain residents of Jerusalem, Bathsheba must have built a wall around her emotions in order to survive. I can see her walking down the corridor, caressing her tummy that held the unborn child and comforting herself, thinking, *They can talk about me all they want and reject me all they please, but at least I have my baby. I will finally have someone to love me unconditionally — a child that will give back to me regardless of circumstances.*

But the baby — a son — died. During the seven days before his child's death, David wept and pleaded for his son, thinking that God might have mercy and change His mind about the fate of the child.

Bathsheba had lost it all. For what? For nothing, it seemed. In the span of one year, she had had an affair, gotten pregnant, been widowed, remarried and lost her baby. She had really blown it. Most of us have things in our past that we would change if we could. But there is nothing to be gained by regrets — only by repentance. Our God is a God of redemption.

## A Wonderful Reward for a Ruined Past

After their son died, David cleaned up, combed his hair and went directly into the house of the Lord to worship. In his agony, he was able to worship the Lord.

To me, his response speaks of maturity. Even though all of this had been the product of his sin, and he was grieving, David worshiped God despite his agony. He said, "God has decided. He has kept me alive to give me another chance to do His will; therefore I will go on."

Do not make the mistake of becoming a long-term sufferer. True, there are times of extended grieving, but at some point we must say, "God is good, God is faithful and He is sovereign. And since He has spoken, I will arise and go on. I refuse to be debilitated emotionally for the rest of my life. Yes, it hurts; yes, it is the most painful thing I have ever endured, but my God is a God of redemption, and in some way I will see His hand for good in all of this."

Something wonderful begins to happen to you when you take your eyes off the past sin and yourself and get them on Jesus. That is the first step toward getting out of the pit.

## Have I Got Good News for You!

David and Bathsheba were given another son, and they named him Solomon. A word came through the prophet Nathan that God had named the baby Jedidiah, which interpreted means "beloved of God" (see 2 Sam. 12:24-25).

What did that baby ever do to make God love him so much? Not a thing. I believe that child was God's overflow of love for the repentant David and Bathsheba. God made their son the second wisest man on the earth. (The wisest, of course, was Jesus.) Their first son died as the result of sin but the last child God put on the throne.

David rejoiced upon his deathbed because he lived to

see his son on the throne. There were many reasons that David chose Solomon above the other sons to inherit the throne of Israel and Judah (see 1 Kin. 1:30). But being the romantic that I am, I wonder if David's choice was because of the love he had for Bathsheba.

## From Shame to Glory

Shortly after Solomon was crowned the new king, Bathsheba, his mother, heard from David's oldest son, Adonijah, who rightfully should have inherited the kingdom. However, God had other ideas. Would Bathsheba be so kind as to speak to her son, King Solomon, on Adonijah's behalf concerning a woman he wanted to marry? She consented to do so.

This part is so cool. Bathsheba entered the room to speak to her son the king. Before she could bow to him, King Solomon jumped up to meet her and bowed at her feet. He then commanded that a throne be set up right beside his so they could sit together. She asked the king if she might make one small request. His reply? "Anything, mother, I will not refuse you anything" (see 1 Kin. 2:13-20).

From being a woman scorned to a woman with authority, from great shame to great glory!

In the book of Proverbs, Solomon wrote about the virtuous woman. This was a description of and tribute to his mother. God did something in Bathsheba's heart that turned her from an adulteress to an example for all women. Solomon had a countless number of wives and concubines. I like to think that he went through a thousand women to find one as wonderful as his mother.

The lessons in this chapter are pretty simple: First, they can apply to marriage or to any area of your life. Take immediate action toward those thoughts that are in disobedience to God's Word. Most of those thoughts can become pretty pleasurable, especially if you are tired, unloved, rejected or just plain bored. This is exactly what the enemy is hoping. He looks for a vulnerable place to attack so that you will justify what you are about to do — inflict a hurt for a hurt. However, sin by retaliation will postpone not only our healing but also the healing of the rest of the innocents.

First, expose the temptation to someone you can trust. Some people can expose their temptations to their mates. Good for you. For some of you, that would not be a good idea. You may find yourself lying flat on the floor with body parts all over the place. In that case, I would recommend finding someone else to confide in. Your mother would be a good choice, unless she has a weak heart. Never get your counsel from the ungodly, because their advice is not based on Word principles (see Ps. 1:1-3).

Second, remember that God is the God of the second chance. We obviously can't run around sinning, repenting, sinning, repenting...you get the picture. We can sure make a mess of our lives sometimes. Sin overtakes us, because when it was chasing us down we just stood there kind of staring at it. Now the results are about to devastate us. That is when we find the grace of God anew.

Just as David did, we can throw ourselves upon His mercy and find forgiveness and restoration.

Thank God, for His mercy endures forever! But please — don't wait that long.

# 13

# Crackers —
# or a Five-Course Meal?

There I was again, complaining to God. Only I didn't feel as if I was complaining. Oh, no — I was simply sharing my thoughts with those around me, particularly on matters concerning my house, the limited amount of bedroom space, the neighbors and on and on. It was not long before the room emptied. The nerve of these people!

But the house was too small. Two babies, complete with cribs, shared our bedroom. In another bedroom were our three two-year-old children. Jerusha, our eighteen-year-old college freshman, had her own bedroom. I tried to talk her into getting bunk beds and sharing her room with her little sister, the same sister who had ruined her last ten lipsticks. I even tried to entice her by offering to decorate the room with matching Pocahontas bedspreads and a coordinating rug and curtains. I can still see the look she gave me — you know, the look that teenagers give you that says, "Are you out of your mind?" A look that let me know her room was non-negotiable...subject closed.

So, when everyone left the room that day, I looked to my precious, loving, heavenly Father for comfort. I wanted Him to console me with words like, "Honey, you are so sweet. I love you so much. You work so hard for me and, bless your little heart, no one in the history of time has worked as hard as you, with the exception of my Son Jesus and your mother."

## Get Off the Floor and Get Out the Door

The Lord did speak to me. He very clearly said, "Why do you behave as a woman who has no covenant?" That was not the response I had expected. He wanted to know why I was speaking and complaining as though I did not have a living God with a living covenant.

I went to my concordance and looked up all the verses on covenant. Out of the sixty-six books of the Bible, reference to the covenant is mentioned in thirty-five books. Covenant, simply put, is a binding pledge, promise, bond, contract or agreement between two people. You can either accept it, passing it from one generation to another, or reject it, but you can never do away with it.

A number of years ago, I enjoyed the friendship of a very dear Christian woman whom I still love and appreciate. We were sisters in the Lord for more than sixteen years. We shared life's joys and sorrows, and we wept with one another, and we laughed together. But a situation arose in the church that forced her to make some choices. Those choices included not returning my phone calls because she was caught in the crossfire of a church dispute. The end result was that hurt feelings, unforgiveness and bitterness

159

destroyed our friendship. I was devastated. Our covenant was broken, and so were our hearts.

Over the years, I had grown very close to her children and grandchildren. We always remembered each other's birthdays and special occasions. The Lord reminded me through His word and the Holy Spirit that I had made a covenant with my friend to remember her children and grandchildren.

With apprehension and even a little self-righteousness — well, a lot of self-righteousness (of which I have since repented) — I obeyed the Lord. I began sending cards and gifts to her family once more. Remembering and honoring my promise to my lost friend has certainly brought tremendous blessings and rewards in my life. There has been a supernatural knitting together of our hearts in spite of the hurt and rejection, and now my friend's daughter and her family are among my dearest friends. She chose to accept the covenant her mother and I had made.

## What's Included in the Ticket Price?

If someone loses a great deal of money and it is returned, it's front-page news — a banner headline just for doing what is right. Many people fail to keep their word today. We have become a generation of covenant-breakers.

A section of our Sunday newspaper is devoted to anniversary and wedding announcements. I live in a fairly large city, and I have noticed that the anniversary announcements take up only about half the page. Couples who actually stay married for fifty years without seriously injuring each other make a newsworthy item. I know a lot of couples that could total the years of all their marriages and come up with one hundred fifty years, but that doesn't count.

Our God is a covenant-keeping God. You can choose to either accept or reject His covenant. As participants in a covenant with God, we are covered by the contract in every area of our lives.

My father used to tell the story of a man who booked passage on a big steamship line from London to New York. He boarded the ship and retired to his cabin, which was below the water line. He took aboard with him enough crackers for as many days as it took to make the voyage. Upon arriving in New York, he came up from his cabin to disembark and was questioned by those around him as to who he was. Upon learning his name, they told him there was a place card at one of the dining tables with his name on it. They just assumed he missed the boat when he didn't appear for any of his meals.

He said, "Oh, no. My ticket only got me passage from London to New York." The others laughed, and one person told him, "Don't you know that when you booked your passage, it also included your meals? You remained in your cabin and ate crackers for two weeks when you could have gone to the dining room and enjoyed three sumptuous meals a day, plus a midnight buffet."

Many live far below their covenant promises, a place where God would love to move and flow in their lives.

## Your Level to Receive Will Never Rise Above Your Level to Believe

Some dear saints believe that their ticket is just for heaven. We need to realize that Jesus gave His life for a ticket that includes everything you need here on earth as well.

Why would you live as though you have no covenant? Why do you live as though you have just enough passage to get by? It's because you do not fully understand the relationship that God desires to have with you.

But I will establish my covenant (promise, pledge)

161

with you, and you shall come into the ark, you, and your sons, and your wife, and your sons' wives with you (Gen. 6:18, AMP).

The ark that God had commanded Noah to build was more than just a floating zoo. It was a symbol of the covenant. Contained in that promise and pledge for Noah was safety, shelter, provision, protection, refuge and preservation of life.

The Word doesn't say too much about Noah's family. It talks primarily about the one man, Noah. However, I believe that all the family was protected by God because of Noah.

Some of you continually cry, "I'm the only one in my family who is serving the Lord." That's great! All you need is one. Thank God there is at least one. I can't emphasize it enough: Why would you behave as if you have no covenant? Why do you fret, worry and cry over family members who do not know the Lord? You have a covenant with God, and it includes your children and your children's children.

## My God Never Lies

God keeps His covenant. He never breaks His word. God blessed Noah and his sons after they came forth from the ark. "And God blessed Noah and his sons, and said to them, 'Be fruitful and multiply, and fill the earth...the sons of Noah who went forth from the ark were Shem, Ham, and Japheth. Ham was the father of Canaan" (Gen. 9:1,18, RSV).

To me, this part of the story gets a little scary. Noah had evidently been locked up a little too long in that ark, so when they set up housekeeping again he built a winepress. He got drunk and was sleeping it off in his tent, and he was — well...naked! "And Ham, the father of Canaan, saw the nakedness of his father, and told his two brothers outside" (Gen. 9:22, RSV).

I don't know exactly what went on in the tent, but Ham must have committed a really huge sin, because when Noah found out what Ham did he was extremely upset. The next thing he did was very interesting. The word says that Noah cursed Canaan, Ham's son. It was Ham that committed the sin, so why did Noah curse Ham's son?

That didn't seem fair. But you see, God had already blessed Ham, and that which God has blessed cannot be cursed.

Do not be afraid of a curse. The word tells us in Proverbs 26:2 that "the curse causeless shall not come" (KJV). God had blessed Ham, and that blessing could not be reversed. Balaam experienced an inability to curse the Israelites when they were under God's covenant — even though a king promised him good money if he would (Num. 22-23).

My husband and I were in a restaurant waiting in line for the cashier to take our money. My husband was sort of singing out loud, and it annoyed a patron in the line behind us. The man looked squarely at Randi and said, "Go to hell." My husband immediately shot back, "I can't." That stranger had cursed him to hell, but the reason Randi told him he couldn't go was because he had a covenant with God. Remember, you cannot curse what God has blessed.

I only wish I could be as witty as he is. If someone said that to me, I would probably start crying and run out because I couldn't think of a thing to say — that is, until I got home.

God can be very specific when He makes a covenant to bless. Look at what He said to Abraham. "On the same day the Lord made a covenant (promise, pledge) with Abram, saying, To your descendants I have given this land, from the river of Egypt to the great river Euphrates" (Gen. 15:18, AMP).

Please take note that God promised land and children to Abraham.

I often hear God's covenant people complain and say,

"I'll never own a house or land. I'm destined to live in this doghouse forever. I could never qualify at the bank even if I did step out and try." You must realize that God set up our covenant, and it includes land. We often long for things that are the very desires placed in us by God. Yet we continue to doubt God's ability to actually bring them to pass.

There are so many couples who come to my meetings and share the agonizing desire to have a child. Please hear me — children are listed as part of your covenant promise.

Mothers and fathers are crying out to God on behalf of their children who have walked away from the Lord. Your children are part of the original covenant given to you. They will walk after the Lord their God, because that is the covenant God has promised to you...land and children.

## Where Do I Sign?

Every contract has a bottom line to it, and a covenant with God is no different. "We will give you this nice bright shiny new automobile for $486.37 a month. But the very minute your due date arrives and you do not give us the $486.37, we will come and tow your shiny new automobile back to the dealership." Every contract has a bottom line, and it costs us something.

Abraham paid the price. It was the price of surrender. He had to surrender everything without the immediate evidence of the reward. This is the point where many believers, with pen in hand, turn away. The covenant, though, requires a yielded heart given in sacrifice, a life that is totally dependent on and submitted to the Father's will.

Now here is more of the good stuff. What's God's part? We sow, water, cry, pray, but it is God who gives the increase (see 1 Cor. 3:6-7). Recently, I have been praying, "Father, I thank You for Your covenant of increase today in my life. I have sown in faith and obedience. I have watered my prayers with tears in the spirit. Now You are responsible for giving the increase to me."

There is no magic wand to wave and then presto, the answer appears. We have witnessed, talked, prodded, preached, confessed but the order still remains the same — God gives the increase.

Do you know that everything God touches multiplies? God continually multiplied Abraham. He was given good, loyal and trusted servants. He was blessed with a good marriage because of the covenant, even though he and Sarah went through some really tough times.

Personally, I think Abraham behaved like a rat at times. He sent his wife to sleep with the king to save his own neck. "Just go ahead honey, tell them you're my sister. It's OK."

Now this is only my opinion, but I also think Abraham went just a little too fast to make a baby with Hagar. Sarah said, "Honey, you could go into my maid Hagar and conceive a child with her."

I could just hear him declining and reluctantly saying, "Oh, I just couldn't. It wouldn't be right. All right, Dear, I'll make the ultimate sacrifice. Be right back."

This marriage suffered a great number of obstacles. However, God blessed the union. After all, didn't Abraham have an active sex life well into his nineties? Now I can just hear some of you saying, "Oh no, please don't tell Herb. He will get his walker and shuffle down to that there Victoria's Secret place and buy me some scary little outfit with a feather boa."

## Covenant Health

Physical healing is part of your covenant. It doesn't matter if you have gone to the doctor, taken all sorts of medication and had all kinds of tests. The bottom line has got to be: When this sickness or infirmity comes to an end, I'm going to be standing on both my feet, totally healed. It is part of my divine right, and I will not sit in my cabin and eat crackers.

Living in Egypt, the Israelites were sick. They were slaves with a slave mentality. They had been overworked and practically starved and had absolutely no idea as to how to go out and possess anything. After they ate of the Passover lamb, death could not touch them. As one body, they walked out of Egypt, and there was not a weak or sickly one among them. God even gave them all the wealth of their wicked oppressors. God's covenant with them included providing the physical stamina they needed to get to the promised land.

## Covenant Power

In Exodus 34:10 we see God making a promise to show us displays of His awesome power. In this hour we have begun to see more and more miracles than ever before.

At a recent meeting I stepped down from the platform to a group of ladies who had gathered for personal ministry. Suddenly their eyes widened as they looked past me, and they began to cry out, "The Lord our God!" As a group, they fell down on their faces and began to worship the Lord. There were no catchers. I didn't even have a chance to pray for them. God just came on the scene in His awesome power. I prophesy to you that in these days we are going to see things that only a privileged few have seen.

## Covenant Favor

God is "leaning toward [us] with favor...establishing and ratifying [His] covenant with [us]" (Lev. 26:9, AMP). To ratify simply means to approve, confirm or guarantee. Favor is part of our covenant promise.

Traveling with my children complicates my life at times.

Babies are really not very mobile individuals. They need six thousand changes of clothes in addition to bottles, formula, bottle warmers, twenty-five thousand pacifiers (only one of which is left in the bottom of the diaper bag at the end of the trip), not to mention diapers, burp rags, baby shampoo, bath gel, moisturizer and the all-important noisy rattle. I like to use the rattle on people seated near me on the airplane who are talking so loud that folks in passing planes can hear them. When I travel with my two bags, a cassette-tape box, a crate of books and seven camels loaded with baby gear, I really need the favor of God.

One time a skycap informed me that I had too many bags. In fact, he told me I had too many bags for fifty people. Trying to explain to him that I really, really, really needed all my stuff did not work. He went inside to talk to the counter manager. Upon returning, he informed me that not only would he check all my bags through, but also the airline would give us VIP treatment. They loaded us on a cart for handicapped people and drove us directly to the gate. Now *that* is the favor of God! He is looking for reasons to grant you favors, and we must respond by putting a demand upon our covenant of favor.

## Covenant Peace

"Behold, I give unto him my covenant of peace" (Num. 25:12). I believe there are some of you reading these words who are desperately in need of the covenant of peace. Your mind races in a million directions. You go to bed, and immediately thoughts begin to pour into your mind: *Did I mail the electric payment? Did I let the cat back in the house this afternoon?* All the things you should have done but had no time to accomplish rush through your mind.

You look in the silverware drawer and see all those little crumbs, and you are overcome with the need to Clorox

167

something. You open the cupboard door and everything falls out. We have a multiple car garage, and yet there are times we can't put the cars in there because of all the junk inside. Sound familiar?

The enemy uses all these things to get our minds going in different directions. Then we get so frustrated that we say, *I think I'll just sit down and have a piece of cheesecake. After that, I'll feel better, and then I'll get started.*

It is in those times you must stop and say, "Father, I step into your covenant of peace right now." All these things are temporary. In the light of eternity, not one soul will care if you had several unidentifiable food particles in your silverware drawer. No one will care if the garage still has four moose heads covered with dust that you promised your husband you would shampoo, blow dry and hang back over the fireplace.

## Covenant Love

Did you know that God has established a covenant of love towards you? "Know therefore that the Lord thy God, he is God, the faithful God, which keepeth covenant and mercy with them that love him and keep his commandments to a thousand generations" (Deut. 7:9).

Why would you behave as though you didn't have a God who was taking care of every detail of your life simply because He loves you? I keep repeating the theme of this chapter to myself: He is a covenant-keeping God. I desperately desire for you to know the type of relationship that our God wants to have with you. Are you lacking in love right now, or are you in a place where dishonor has come or in a marriage where love has disappeared because of numerous angry words and hurts? Perhaps you are single — you have given everything you can emotionally give and still do not feel loved. I want to tell you that He has made an everlasting covenant of love with you. It is a love that will not fail. It's not like man's love. There is not one thing that you could possibly do or not do that can make the Father love you any more than He loves you at this very moment.

## All I Want Is Everything

In the early Old Testament times, God had given man a place of prominence in government and in the tabernacle and as the beneficiary of the laws of inheritance. If a man died, everything went to his sons. If that man had no sons, his inheritance was passed on to his closest male relative.

Women, on the other hand, were good for cleaning, cooking, bearing children, keeping the tent tidy and so forth. However, there is an incident in Numbers 27 in which five women changed God's mind. Five persistent, intelligent women changed history for generations that followed.

"Then came the daughters of Zelophehad...The names of his daughters: Mahlah, Noah, Hoglah, Milcah, and Tirzah" (Num. 1:27, AMP). Just between us, I think that Hoglah was the homely one. She was the one who had to keep the veil over her face. You know the routine: "Marry her, she has a great personality" — that's what her father might have said.

The Word tells us that these daughters were the great-great-great-great-great granddaughters of Joseph. They knew their heritage. They knew that Joseph had a covenant with God based on his father Isaac's covenant with God. That meant that they too shared in their father's inheritance. So why were all of their father's land and possessions being given over to a distant relative, just because they were girls and their father had no son?

These five daughters presented themselves at the door of the tent of meeting and faced Moses, Eleazar the priest and the entire congregation and stated their case.

Our father died in the desert. He was not among

Korah's followers, who banded together against the Lord, but he died for his own sin and left no sons. Why should our father's name disappear from his clan because he had no son? Give us property among our father's relatives" (Num. 27:3-4, NIV).

Moses, great man of power and anointing, prophet of the Most High, didn't have a clue as to what to do with them. Moses told everyone that he would be right back and went to inquire of the Lord. "Lord, what shall I do?"

The Lord's answer: "They have asked a good thing. Give them their portion of the inheritance. Not only that, but I am going to establish what they have asked as a precedent."

Do you realize that they never would have received if they had not appealed? They would not have received anything if they had not put a demand on the covenant. They didn't know what God *would* do, but they knew what God *could* do.

Many precious believers are living below their covenant blessing and promises simply because they do not realize the abundant overflowing and passionate love that their heavenly Father has stored up for them.

A woman of God once shared a dream in which the Lord had come to her in heaven. Jesus took her to a room filled to capacity with beautifully wrapped gifts of all sizes. She asked Jesus, "Are these my rewards?"

"No," He sadly replied. "These were all the blessings and answers to prayers and gifts that I had for you when you were on earth, but you never asked for them."

# 14

# Just When You Thought You'd Seen It All

I was raised in a Pentecostal church, the daughter of a Pentecostal father/pastor in a non-traditional Pentecostal home (that meant we *could* go swimming without having to wear culottes and a turtleneck sweater). I thought I had pretty much seen and heard everything.

I lived through multiple two-week revivals and six summers of church camp, and, because my parents were pastors, I saw scores of really strange evangelists. You know, the ones with really poufy hair that starts with a gigantic pointy pompadour on the forehead and combs straight back from there in a greasy dark-brown wave. Plus the evangelists had the privilege of sleeping in *my* bed, in *my* room, while I got to sleep on the couch.

I remember my parents taking me to the huge tent crusades

where Oral Roberts was performing miracles by the Holy Spirit. Of course, I was only four years old, and I couldn't see very far even when standing on a chair. In fact, maybe Oral Roberts wasn't really there, and they just told me that because actually we were at the movies, and back then it was a huge, I mean really huge, sin to go to the picture show.

In 1976, I met this really great messianic Jew who had no Pentecostal training whatsoever, and the responsibility on me to train him was enormous, except for the small fact that he had a much greater revelation of the Holy Spirit than I did. He introduced me to many great teachers such as Bob Mumford, Don Basham, Derek Prince, and Roy and Pauline Harthern. I had never heard such revelation of the Word. They could take a single scripture and preach for two hours in a sort of monotone; yet we were glued to our chairs, not wanting to miss a single word.

That precious man became my husband. Shortly after we were married, he decided it was time for further training and announced that we were going to a meeting where Derek Prince was speaking. It was a deliverance service.

"A what?" I asked.

He repeated, "A deliverance service."

"Are you implying that I perchance need deliverance? Well, I don't, and even if I did, I don't believe in that kind of stuff because we certainly did not have that sort of thing in *our* Pentecostal church. Don't come near me, or I will scream!" I said.

Two hours later, we were sitting in the back row of the meeting listening to the Word of God being preached when the man of God began to pray for people right where they were sitting. He didn't shout, he didn't scream, he just commanded fear and oppression to leave God's people. I knew I was witnessing God at work.

That was the start of my training. But it was only recently

that I had an experience with the Holy Spirit that has forever removed the "been there, done that" attitude from my soul.

## My Relationship to God

I never fully understood the full meaning of a "renewal conference" until recently, when I accepted an invitation to be the speaker at one such meeting in Sunderland Christian Centre in England.

After that conference, I could truly say that I would never be the same. It impacted my life forever. I hope I can make it as real to you as it was to me. This is not your ordinary missionary report where I show slides and, "click, click," I produce a picture of Bubba, our guide in the wilderness, and "click, click," the mud hut we lived in and "click, click," a slide of the three people that got saved.

Do you remember those missionary Sundays? At the end they would ask, "Who wants to go?" I thought, *Who wants to go? No one I know is going to want to give up sitting in their green recliner to go over there and live in a hut and sit on the ground and eat mosquito legs.* Then they got to the part when they asked, "Who will give?" We were all glad to give, just so we didn't have to go. Of course, that's what they were counting on.

Like most of you, I thought I had seen it, done it, been through every new move of God there is and now — what's left to see? I've laughed, cried, fallen under the power of God and seen visions. I've seen the Word of Faith movement, the teaching movement, the prophetic movement, the healing movement and all the rest.

I have ministered all over the world, and I've witnessed many things. But as I was preparing to go to England, the Lord said to me, "You are going to be part of something historical." It wasn't that I was going to make history; I was just going to be a part of something that God was going to do on a grander scale than I could possibly imagine. I was so thrilled that the Lord would speak those words to me. I was filled with anticipation at what He was going to do.

When we arrived in the little town of Sunderland, through the Spirit of God I could sense an excitement. The pastor, Ken Gott, and his wife, Lois, took me to dinner that first night so we could get acquainted. I recognized Lois from a meeting I held in Winter Park, Florida.

As we drove to dinner, they went by one area very slowly and said, "Here's the place where the vicar's wife laid hands on Smith Wigglesworth, and he was baptized in the Holy Spirit with fire." Outside the church was a plaque that read, "Here is the place where the fire fell and burned up all the death." Smith Wigglesworth, who lived from 1859-1947, was a great British evangelist known for his unwavering faith and healing ministry.

Please note that I am not a "woo-woo" sort of person. I have a husband who keeps my feet planted firmly on the ground. However, as we drove past this church, the power of God sovereignly fell on me as I sat in the back seat of the car. I felt absolutely foolish, because I couldn't sit up straight in my seat. I felt as if there were a hand on the side of my head pushing me down. The anointing of God was strong.

I was hungry for more of the things of God. He said He would take us from glory to glory to glory to glory. If you continue to stay on the bottom level, you'll begin to stagnate and you will never get to the next level of glory.

I was sitting in the car, trying to stay composed, when Lois asked me if I remembered the word I gave her when she attended my Winter Park meeting. I told her that I was sorry I didn't. Then she surprised me by stating that I was in England as a result of what God did for her that day. She could sense I was having a problem remembering all the Lord had said to her through the prophetic word, so she took sheets of paper from her purse and began to read the prophecy to me.

She had come to the meeting with a pastor's wife whom I had never met. She explained, "In that meeting I was thinking, *These poor Americans, they're so gullible and will believe anything.* Then you called out my friend from the congregation and, not knowing who she was, you spoke prophetically to her of the things we had sat up all night talking about. All of a sudden, you had my attention. Then you said you had a word for a woman from England. You prophesied to me that what the enemy meant for evil to destroy me, God was going to turn around for good."

She continued, "I had lost a baby son, and it nearly destroyed me. I was an emotional wreck." The Lord spoke to her through the prophetic word and said, "Go home and tell the man of God that the building is too small." She couldn't believe it! They had just finished a new sanctuary that seated 950, even though their congregation consisted of only 150 people. It was built at great sacrifice on the part of the congregation. The word went on to say how the devil tried everything within his power to keep them from occupying the building. But the word of the Lord said, "Daughter, I am going to come in that place and visit it. People will come from around the world to see what I am doing in that building."

She went home and told Ken what she had received. His attitude was, "Oh yeah, right!" Everyone had sold all their possessions to build this new sanctuary, and then the Gotts were to tell them it was too small? "We just didn't bear witness that it was God," she said.

The English are very staid people. Nothing much can move them, Lois told me. But one day Ken was standing behind the pulpit when the power of God came upon him so strongly that it was impossible for him to stand. This happened thirty days after she shared with him what God had said to her through the prophetic word. He said to his congregation, "If you want what God is putting on me, run to the front." With that, he fell under the mighty power of God, taking the pulpit down with him.

People started to run to the front of the sanctuary. Before they could get to the altar, they fell in the aisles under the power of God. I wept as she told this to me. Inside of me I was crying, "Oh, God, I don't have this, and I want it."

I wondered, *How do I get this? Where do I sign up? What tape series do I buy? What vow do I pledge?* Americans are so used to doing "things" to get what we want. But God began to show me a side of Himself that said, "I'm God; you're not. Watch out!"

When I got back to the hotel, I called together the ladies who had accompanied me from the States. I tried to tell them all that I had just heard as we wept and rejoiced together.

When I was alone, I said to God, "I'm really intimidated by the anointing that they have in this place. What do they need me for? Why did You bring me here? I am really going to look stupid compared to all these others who have such an anointing. They probably won't understand any of my funny stories, and I will fall flat."

I felt as if the Spirit of the Lord pulled me up by my ears and said, "If I had wanted to do what I have always been doing, I would not have had them send for you. They are ready for the prophetic, and I have brought you here to give the word of the Lord in order to take them to the next step." He instructed me not to be intimidated.

Do you know that intimidation is fear? And the root of fear is pride. And pride has much to do with your image. The Lord let me know that this experience was going to bring a death to my image and pride.

The next day, Ken told me that when he was in prayer for this conference two weeks prior to my coming, the Lord asked him, "Son, are you ready for the prophets? I am send-ing the prophets. Get ready." It was a confirmation of what God had spoken to me.

Lois told me that ever since the prophetic word came, they had had church every night of the week for thirteen months prior to my coming. She said several hundred attended every night.

## At Least God Didn't Ask for My Makeup

As I was preparing for the first evening service, the Lord spoke to me and said, "Cathy, take off your jewelry." He has never said that to me before. I thought I didn't hear Him right, because it seemed like such a silly thing. I asked the Lord why. He directed me to Exodus 38:8, which describes the instructions for building the tabernacle for the Lord. "And he made the laver of bronze and its base of bronze, from the mirrors of the ministering women who ministered at the door of the tent of meetings" (RSV).

The laver was a huge basin that held water for the priest to purify himself before he served the Lord in the temple. The laver was made from the mirrors. And what did the mirrors represent? Their image, their vanity and what they wanted other people to see in them. And who brought them? The women who ministered. They melted them to make the laver, which was used for purification and cleansing.

That is why the Lord spoke to me in my hotel room and said, "Take off all your jewelry, because you are getting ready to enter into a holy place. It is not your image I want the people to see. I don't want them to see your glory, your gift or your anointing. I want them to see *my* glory, *my* gift, *my* anointing and *my* image."

As I started to take off my jewelry, I looked in the mirror. I never realized how plain I looked without it. I was accus-tomed to seeing myself with earrings, necklace and rings.

177

The Lord had me remove even my wedding rings. In obedience, I stripped myself of all adornment.

Taking my jewelry off was simply symbolic of what the Lord wanted to do in me and with me before the people. He was going to melt my image.

I remember calling to ask what the dress for the meetings was going to be. The answer was, "Who cares?" We here in America want to know if it is casual, dressy casual, semi-dressy, jogging suits, blue jeans. They said, "We don't care what you wear. Just come. When the anointing is present, no one really cares what you have on." All of a sudden, things I thought were so important seemed rather trite.

God is going to require our mirrors. He's not asking just to borrow them. He's asking to change them permanently.

## Encounter with God in Merry Old England

I have never been in a sanctuary where I could not stand up because the power of God was so strong. When I walked into Sunderland Christian Centre I grabbed hold of a table to keep from falling down while I tried to gain my composure. I had to hold on to pews as I walked up the aisle. The anointing of God was so powerful, I wanted to bow and cover my face.

Praise and worship had already begun, and the congregation was singing about the Lord of the dance. Everyone was worshiping! It didn't take twenty minutes of praise and worship to get them in the spirit. They were in the spirit already. They began to sing the old hymns of the church that I love so much, only I had never heard them sung that way before. When they sang "All hail the power of Jesus' name, let angels prostrate fall," you could hear the angels dropping in that place. Never have I been in a meeting where there was such a tangible presence of God.

Pastor Ken related to me that in one of the meetings a little

178

boy about four years old came to him and said, "I have something I want to say." When the pastor let him speak, he said, "An angel just came in, and he's standing over there."

The pastor asked him how he knew.

"Because he's standing this far off the ground," he said, indicating with his hand about three feet above the floor.

The pastor asked him, "When did he come in?"

The little boy answered, "Pastor, there have been angels all around this place all night. But when the golden angel came in, all the other angels covered their faces and bowed down. Can't you see him? He's right over there. He's touching people, and they're getting healed." When he said that, people all around began falling down under the power and the anointing of the Spirit of God and were being healed.

It was not man's glory, not man's hand. It was just the sovereign work of the Holy Spirit.

The church holds 950. They crammed one thousand people into the sanctuary with standing room only, and they turned at least one thousand people away because there was no more room. Now the pastor understood why God told him the sanctuary was too small.

You see, God always prophesies about what's around the corner. Some say prophecy is only for confirmation. Sometimes when the word comes out of the mouth of His prophet, it's not confirmation — it's stuff you never even heard. God is speaking through the mouth of His servants, the prophets, to prepare you for what He is getting ready to do. Don't doubt the word.

During the meeting, Lois asked a delegation from Scotland to stand. They all stood up. Then, with a slight wave of her arm she said, "Bless the ladies from Scotland, Lord." When she did that, down went the whole delegation from Scotland. There they lay on the floor with their cute little sweaters, purses dangling on their arms and gray hair turned under like the queen mother. They went down under the power of God, kilts and all. I thought, *There goes our bagpipe special.*

The effects of those meetings could not be contained within the church walls.

In the city of Sunderland crime had escalated due to the unemployment that resulted when the local shipyards were closed. Car theft was the number one method of earning a living. The month that renewal started in the church, crime dropped 40 percent, and car theft dropped 66 percent.

One particular young woman came to the church and got saved and filled with the Holy Spirit. Her boyfriend was a murderer, a pimp, head of the prostitution ring and one of the best-known crime lords in the city. This renewal that had come into the city was destroying his business, and he was mad. To top it off, his girlfriend got saved. He had it in for the pastor. One night he walked up the aisle of the church during the altar call and headed straight for the pastor with the intention of punching his lights out. Ken Gott was not a big man compared to the boyfriend — who was huge. You know, he had the kind of arms that stick out on either side because of the enormous muscles. And it wasn't fat...just pure muscle.

Ken closed his eyes, expecting to be clobbered. Jim, the big guy, pulled his fist back and was ready to hit Ken when the power of God came and socked him in the jaw and knocked him to the ground. He got up two hours later, saved and filled with the Holy Spirit. He gave his testimony before everyone. He said, "I used to be a murderer. Some of the things I have done, I can't even describe. But Jesus has changed my life."

Religion didn't do it! It was Jesus. *He* changed his life. Jim came under conviction for the life he had lived and married his girlfriend. Now they're working in the church and serving God together in the house of the Lord in Sunderland.

As I spoke one Sunday morning, in the middle of the message the Lord gave me a prophecy for Ken. He said, "There will be many, many men of God that are going to come to this place. They will come with their collars buttoned up under their chin and their ties fastened tightly. They will be stiff-necked, religious, opinionated and critical when they come. I am going to use you to teach them and minister the life of God. They will begin to unbutton their buttons and pull off their ties."

My eyes were closed as I spoke these words, so I was not aware that Ken Gott, who was sitting on the front row, had been pantomiming what I was saying.

I opened my eyes and saw Ken had unbuttoned his shirt, removed his tie and pitched it over his shoulder into the congregation. I was amazed as I saw the tie float out over three rows of people, as if it were carried by a puff of air. Everyone in its path fell down under the power and anointing of God.

I saw manifestations of the Holy Spirit such as I have never before witnessed. I went from group to group of people standing in line for prayer, and before I could lay hands on them and pray for them, they would fall down under the power of God.

This church is part of a particular denomination which, when they found out all that was going on, decided to shut Sunderland down and strip Ken of his ministerial papers. After all, people were getting saved and delivered and the church was growing, so it could not possibly be God! We've never done it this way before, and they are on the fringe, and someone has to put a stop to it. The director of this denomination came from his headquarters to hold a special meeting to close the church. He took the microphone in his hand and opened his mouth to rebuke the pastor and his congregation when God struck him dumb.

He tried to speak, but no words would come out. God

would not let him talk. God will not let His glory be stopped in the earth. Do you think man could stop what God wants to do? At that point, the power of God knocked this man to the floor. When he got up he was crying and asked if they would bring what they had to Australia. The Gotts later travelled to Australia to take the anointing and renewal of the Spirit of the Lord to that part of the world.

I thought of the lyrics of a hit song from the sixties: "Then I saw her face; now I'm a believer. There's not a trace of doubt in my mind." When you see His face, you become a believer! I was seeing new levels of God's miraculous power I never knew existed until now.

We haven't arrived yet, no matter how far we've come. He has greater things planned for us than we can ever imagine.

As God's glory comes, I don't want to be sitting in the outer courts, looking at myself in a mirror. I want to press into the holy place and encounter Him.

As my time at the Sunderland church came to a close, I had been humbled as far as I thought I could go. Then Ken Gott said that he had a word from the Lord for me.

# 15

# Don't Ask for the Window Seat

I get a lot of prophetic words. Some I witness to, and some are really weird. However, the word I received in England was so awesome, it's difficult for me to talk about it.

It was prefaced by a story from 2 Samuel that tells about the ark of the covenant being stolen by the Philistines. God allowed the ark to be stolen to symbolize the spiritual state of Israel. What did the ark of the covenant represent? The presence of God. Now it was gone.

The ark was returned to the Israelites, and it rested on a threshing floor for a while. Then King David decided to bring it back into the city. David was thrilled, because the most important thing to him was the presence of the Lord.

> So David went and brought up the ark of God
> from the house of Obed-edom to the city of David
> with rejoicing (2 Sam. 6:12, RSV).

Why did they rejoice? Because the presence of God was
coming back into the city of David.

Have you ever been without the presence of God? Has
there ever been a time in your life when you knew you had
grieved the Spirit of the Lord? Not unto everlasting damna-
tion — but you did or said something that you knew
grieved Him, and you knew the presence of the Lord wasn't
with you as it used to be.

The Israelites were happy because the presence of God
was back. When they walked six paces, they sacrificed an
ox and fatlings. One, two, three, four, five, six, "OK, everyone stop. We're going to make a sacrifice unto the Lord."

When you are in the presence of the Lord you want to
give, you want to sow. When I was in the renewal meetings
in Sunderland, all I wanted to do was give. I had English
pound notes, and I had no idea what I was giving; I just
wanted to give it to the Lord. You cannot be in the presence
of the Lord and not have a spirit of giving. When God is
present, you do things that you would not normally do.

> And David danced before the Lord with all his
> might; and David was girded with a linen ephod.
> So David and all the house of Israel brought up
> the ark of the Lord with shouting, and with the
> sound of the trumpet (2 Sam. 6:14).

The presence of the Lord was coming! When the presence of the Lord comes, who cares about anything else?
The Israelites canceled work that day because the presence
of the Lord was coming. My prayer is, "Oh, God, don't let
Your presence depart from me. I can live without a lot of
stuff, but I cannot live without Your presence." I don't want

just a visitation from God. A visitation would mean He wasn't there before, and He is going to leave again. I want Him to reside in my life.

The word continues, "As the ark of the Lord came into the city of David, Michal Saul's daughter looked through a window, and saw king David leaping and dancing before the Lord; and she despised him in her heart" (2 Sam. 6:16).

The window is where the religious folks sit. The window is where the critics and judges sit. They are not a part of what's going on. They are not a part of the dance and the worship. They're not even worshiping God in their own way. They're just sitting in the window judging everyone else.

Michal was the daughter of the first king. She knew proper protocol and etiquette because she had been raised in the palace. She knew how worship should be done, and she looked down on David because he stripped off his kingly robes and danced before the Lord. If you didn't know who was king, you couldn't tell him from anyone else. Michal was a symbol of the professional church.

In our Christian circles, we set up kings today. Then, when they act like kings, we become critical of them. God is looking for just a voice that will be used for Him. This is the hour when God is raising up "nobodies," when no one is the king except the King.

Michal sat in the window and was critical. *We don't do it that way,* she no doubt thought.

I was raised in a Pentecostal church and heard people stand before the congregation and say something like, "I'm going to sing a special number today. I haven't practiced and I don't know the words very well, and my pianist has only one arm and is blind, but you just pray for me as I sing that it may be a blessing to you."

We got away from that foolishness when we caught the revelation that God is looking for excellence. However, there is a big difference between excellence and what

Michal had. She was the picture of the professional. She was the professional worshiper. She knew the liturgy. She knew all the right things to do. But David was down in the street cutting loose with the Spirit of God, and he didn't care what anyone thought.

Michal was thinking, *That is not the way we do it. It must be done decently and in order.* Often when some people say that, all they have is *order.* They aren't *doing* anything at all. Some of our churches have moved in that direction. We don't want to offend some rich person and drive them away. We have to get it all coordinated so that the yuppies will come. I know of a church that changed the color of their walls and the color of their tithing envelopes because a consultant said it would make people give more.

When I was growing up, I was reluctant to bring my friends to church because there was always some dear sister who would get the word of the Lord, and if you were sitting in front of her, her voice would knock your wig off. Everything would be very quiet and she would give the word out with such a loud, screeching voice that you couldn't hear what she was saying because your heart was pounding so loud.

We were embarrassed, but now it seems we have so much order, we order Jesus right out. The story is told of a poorly dressed man, standing in front of a church looking very depressed. Jesus stood beside him and asked him what was wrong. He said, "They won't let me in." Jesus replied, "That's all right. They won't let Me in either."

There can be no move of the Spirit in some churches because we haven't given the Lord any time. We may wait for a few minutes after we sing our "slow" song to see if there is a prophetic word. Then we move on quickly to the offering and then the sermon so we can get everybody out by noon. If the service lasts any longer people won't come back.

We have to get to the place where we want God to be

God, and we don't care how long it takes. There is no set time that tells us how long to stay and worship, just as there is no law that says you have to fall down when you are prayed for.

As I was returning from my trip to England, the Spirit of the Lord spoke to me and said, "Revival is coming to America." I know we have heard that religious rhetoric for years: "Revival is coming! Revival is here!" I know for certain that if revival were here, there wouldn't be any empty pews in the church. People would have to get there early to get a seat. Neither the weather nor the way their kids felt would determine whether or not they would go to church. They'd just go.

> And they brought in the ark of the Lord, and set it
> in his place (2 Sam. 6:17).

When the Israelites brought in the ark, they already had a place prepared for it. Some of you have been weeping as you read this, because you are already prepared for what God is going to do. David had already prepared a place for the glory before it arrived.

I could see David getting in Michal's face and telling her, "It was before the Lord." He didn't dance for the people. David was the amateur; Michal was the professional. "It was before the Lord, who chose me before thy father," David pointed out. She wanted him to do things the way her father did. But God did not want that type of king anymore. "Therefore will I play before the Lord" (2 Sam. 6:21).

## Not Michal, Please!

When Ken Gott called me to the front so he could deliver what God gave him for me, he began by reading 2 Samuel. I thought, *Oh, Lord, please don't let me be Michal.* But the word that came forth was, "Cathy, I called you to be David. I called you to be an amateur. You'll never be a professional. You'll always be simple. You'll always be childlike. Never become a Michal. There will be people that will say, 'If you will do it this way, you'll have more finances with which to do more,' but I have called you to be an amateur." An amateur is usually someone who is short on ability but long on perseverance.

There were other things that he said, but to me they are too holy and too precious for me to tell. I have almost worn out that tape listening to it. I know I'll always be an amateur. Oh yes, I've tried to do the professional thing, but it just doesn't work for me.

Do you know what that word of the Lord did for me? *It set me free.* It let me know that I don't have to try to fit in a particular ministry image. I was liberated from the bronze mirror that reflects my own image. The fact is, God is looking for a people who do not want their own image, but His. All I want to do is glorify the King.

I was in a meeting at my home church, and I wanted to sing a chorus which I thought went like this: "If you can use a donkey you can use me." I was trying to get everyone to sing and wondered why they looked at me strangely and would not join in. I was singing my little heart out, "If you can use a donkey you can use me. Use my mouth, Lord, let me bray; use my hooves, Lord, and I will pray. If you can use a donkey you can use me."

This service was being broadcast over the radio, so I urged the people, "Come on, sing with me, 'If you can use a donkey.' I felt someone nudge me and heard our minister of music say, 'Psst, Psst, Cathy — it's if you can use anything.'"

Michal told David that she despised him and that the maids who danced with him despised him as well. For most of his life, no one esteemed David. Not even his own father considered him king material. But by revelation David responded, "By these slave girls you spoke of, I will be held in honor" (2 Sam. 6:21, NIV). Those maids would recognize the new anointing.

Michal, the daughter of Saul, had no child until the day of her death. Her one-sentence rebuke of her husband resulted in a miserable existence for the rest of her days. God had cursed her womb. Why? Ezekiel 16:44 says, "As is the mother, so is her daughter." God did not want the spirit of Michal to continue to a new generation. I wonder if David ever slept with Michal again after she tried to emasculate him.

If you are not ready for the move of God, that's OK. "Deep calls to deep" (Ps. 42:7, RSV). God will give you that hunger when you are ready to ask for it. But don't sit in the window and despise the works of the Lord.

So here we are, just a bunch of amateurs who love God. We aren't perfect, but we've been called, chosen and set apart. To what purpose? To strengthen people's relationships with a loving God who yearns for them and to build up our relationships with one another.

The last part of the prophetic word that was given to me was the most precious message I have ever received from God. Ken told me that God was stretching the wineskin (see Luke 5:37-38). That sounds really painful, but I know from experience that it is true. He continued to say that He had to stretch the wineskin, because in my present condition I could not contain the new wine that He was pouring out in my life. Wherever I would go, I would be a vessel to take this wine to a thirsty and hurting people.

I lay on the floor in northern England on that September evening and wept until there were no more tears. I wept for the nations, and I wept for relationships in my life that are still in conflict.

As I left the church that night, I purposed in my heart to clean up any mess I may have made by not doing what was right in the sight of God. I'll let you know next time how it all turned out.

Covenant Ministries would like to recommend the
following taped messages by Cathy Lechner:

### Single Tape Messages

The Faces of Fear
If You Can Be Offended, You Will Be
If You Are Not Praying, Quit Complaining!
Rejection and Betrayal
Lessons in the Wilderness
How to be a Line-Crosser
Abigail — Living With Difficult Men and Angry People
Why Has My Brook Dried Up?
Why Does It Still Bother You If You've Died to Self?
Crackers or a Five-course Meal?
The Impending Birth of the Promise
The Dream Thieves
Always Reaching Higher
Twisters — The Wind of Deliverance
Breaking the Heart of God

### Tape Series

Women of God (Two tapes)
Rejection (Two tapes)
Becoming God's Hero (Three tapes)

Single tapes cost $6 each, the two-tape series are $12 each,
and the three-tape series are $18 each.

Shipping and handling charges are as follows: orders $0-$6 add
$1.50; $6.01-$30 add $3; over $30 add 10 percent of total order.

Please send your order along with a check
or money order in U.S. funds to:

Covenant Ministries
P.O. Box 17097
Jacksonville, FL 32216
(904) 641-9880

If you enjoyed *Couldn't We Just Kill 'em and Tell God They Died?*, we would like to recommend Cathy's best-seller.

## *I'm Trying to Sit at His Feet, But Who's Going to Cook Dinner?*

Do the demands of marriage, motherhood, finances and career seem never-ending? In the face of life's pressures, many women pull away from God. Buried in stacks of laundry, they say they can't take it anymore, and they forget the promises and purpose God has for their lives.

In Cathy Lechner's national best-seller, *I'm Trying to Sit at His Feet, But Who's Going to Cook Dinner?*, she ministers with humor and prophetic anointing to women across the country.

In the midst of your pressure situation, Cathy shows you how to walk in peace as God's Holy Spirit reveals His purposes for your life. Cathy's hilarious anecdotes and side-splitting stories will set you free and release the joy of the Lord in you.

Available at your local Christian bookstore or from:

Creation House
600 Rinehart Road
Lake Mary, FL 32746
1-800-283-8494
Web site: http://www.creationhouse.com